W9-AAF-090

Advance Praise for Tony Magee's
CAN'T SHOVE A GREAT LIFE INTO A SMALL DREAM!

"My friend, you've got great dreams and Tony wants you to transform them into extraordinary greatness within this book!"

> —**Mark Victor Hansen**, Co-Creator of New York Times Bestselling Book Series, *Chicken Soup for the Soul*® and *The One Minute Millionaire*

"Tony Magee's *Can't Shove a Great Life into a Small Dream* is a great book full of practical advice for everyday people who want to achieve their dreams."

> —**Jack Canfield**, Co-Creator of New York Times Bestselling Book Series, *Chicken Soup for the Soul*®

"*Can't Shove a Great Life into a Small Dream* will inspire you to challenge yourself to live your best life, both personally and professionally. Tony's book of self-discovery will change your life forever."

> —**Les Brown**, Best Selling Author of *Live Your Dreams* and *It's Not Over Until You Win*

"*Can't Shove a Great Life into a Small Dream* is filled with love, wit and good sense. The book began to change my life from the very first chapter."

> —**Joseph C. Phillips,** *Actor, Commentator*

"Everyone has a dream, and in order to live your dream you've got to wake up! Tony Magee's book *Can't Shove a Great Life into a Small Dream* outlines 12 key elements of highly successful people. Read it for prosperity and achieve your dreams."

> —**Dottie Walters**, Co-Author of *Speak and Grow Rich*

"How big is your dream? Read Tony's book *Can't Shove a Great Life into a Small Dream,* and I promise you it will be bigger!"

> —**W Mitchell**, Author of *It's Not What Happens To You, It's What You Do About It!*

i

"Can't Shove a Great Life into a Small Dream will inspire you to be better, motivate you to have more, and encourage you to give more. Tony's book is a winner!"

> **—Nido R. Qubein,** *Chairman,*
> *Great Harvest Bread Company*

"Tony has told a story that is powerful in its lessons, fascinating in its mileposts, and enduring in its guidance through life's unexpected turns. The reading is superbly tailored to appeal to everyone who has always wondered how yesterday's sunset blooms into today's promises."

> **—David Uru Iyam, PhD,** *Associate Professor of*
> *Anthropology, Whittier College, California*

"Tony Magee is an incredible spirit. His book *Can't Shove a Great Life into a Small Dream* is a fabulous piece of work! It's definitely a page-turner. You'll love it too."

> **—Carolyn Kalil**, Author of *Follow Your True Colors*
> *To The Work You Love*

"The experiences and life-lessons presented in *Can't Shove a Great Life into a Small Dream* are awesome and should be shared with everyone that wants to win in life. Tony motivates his readers and makes them come alive!!!"

> **—Amanda H. Goodson, PhD,** Author of *Zero Gravity:*
> *Reach for the Stars!*

"Tony Magee is a friend and a leader on a mission to provide food for thought to fellow would-be leaders. Chapter by chapter, this book *Can't Shove a Great Life into a Small Dream* is filled with reflective anecdotes and thought teasers for readers and leaders of all ages. Word by word, Tony offers a reminder to each of us to be mindful of our responsibilities— to ourselves and to others."

> **—Bill Bellows, PhD,** Expert Business Strategist,
> *The Boeing Company*

"Can't Shove a Great Life into a Small Dream is a book of simple life concepts with profound meaning. It is a must read for anyone who is serious about success!"

> —**Willie Jolley**, Author of *It Only Takes a Minute To Change Your Life* & *A Setback Is a Setup for a Comeback!*

"Can't Shove a Great Life into a Small Dream not only teaches you how to take your goal pursuit from zero to sixty, but how to nurture, sustain and maintain your dream. This book will help a lot of people."

> —**Karen Ragland Cole, MD, MPH, MBA,** *Stanford University*

"Clever, sensitive and life-changing work from Tony! This book is for those ranging from the ghetto streets to Wall Street. A must read for anyone looking to make major changes in their life."

> —**James Dubose**, *Popular Television Producer*

"Tony Magee is passionate and speaks from the heart as he helps us to achieve our dreams! He reaches out and lifts us up in his inspirational book—*Can't Shove a Great Life into a Small Dream!"*

> —**Cathy McClure**, Director, Su Casa Family Crisis Center, Los Angeles, California

"Tony, this is a really good book. *Can't Shove a Great Life into a Small Dream* has powerful lessons in it that will encourage anyone to get rid of their many convenient excuses and live their dreams."

> —**Tim Story**, Director of No. 1 box-office hit movie, *Barbershop*

CAN'T
SHOVE A
GREAT
LIFE
INTO A
SMALL
DREAM™

CAN'T
SHOVE A
GREAT
LIFE
INTO A
SMALL
DREAM™

12 Life-Essentials™ to Grow Your Dreams to Match the Life You Want

TONY MAGEE, MS, MBA

platinumstar
PUBLISHING

Can't Shove a Great Life into a Small Dream™
12 Life-Essentials™ to Grow Your Dreams to Match the Life You Want

© 2003 by Tony Magee, MS, MBA

All rights reserved. This book may not be reproduced in whole or in part without written permission from the publisher, except by a reviewer who may quote brief passages in an article or a review; nor may any part of this book be reproduced, stored in a retrieval system, or transmitted in any form or by any means, electronic, mechanical, photocopying, recording, or other, without written permission from the publisher.

Trademarks appearing in the book are the property of their respective owners and are used only to identify them and/or their respective products and services.

Can't Shove a Great Life into a Small Dream™, Life-Essentials™, The Destiny Doctor™ and PlatinumStar™ are all trademarks owned by Tony Magee, MS, MBA.

Printed in the United States of America.

10 9 8 7 6 5 4 3 2

ISBN 0-9728534-0-5

Editors: Robin Quinn and Jack Barnard

Back and Flap Copywriting by Susan Kendrick and Graham Van Dixhorn

Cover and Book Design by Dunn+Associates

PlatinumStar Publishing
Woodland Hills, California 91365
www.platinumstar.com

Publisher's Cataloging-in-Publication

Magee, Tony.
    Can't shove a great life into a small dream : 12
life-essentials to grow your dreams to match the life
you want / Tony Magee.
    p. cm.
    ISBN 0-9728534-0-5

    1. Success--Psychological aspects. 2. Success in
business. 3. Self-esteem. 4. Change (Psychology)
5. Self-actualization (Psychology)   I. Title.

BF637.S8M34 2003   158
                           QBI33-1442

DEDICATION

To my beloved mother Novel Jean Taplin-Magee
for giving me life, love, wisdom and happiness.

To my Grandmother Mattie Marie Taplin for always believing
in me, for all the times I didn't believe in myself.

To my best friend and wife Aloria
for making all my dreams come true.

To my brilliant children Stephanie, Ahsaan, and Ahmir;
remember, you can, if you think you can!

To all youth who are headed for a life marked by violence
and poverty; keep in mind that it's a contradiction to be
human and not have a special gift to offer service to others.

ACKNOWLEDGMENTS

Throughout my life I have shared a bond with so many people who have supported me both personally and professionally. The many life-lessons learned have been channeled into this book. I wish to thank my friends in the National Speakers Association, Mark Victor Hansen, Jack Canfield, Dottie Walters, Les Brown, Nido Qubein, Joe and Carol Bonura, Marilyn Sherman, Stedman Graham, Willie Jolley, Tracy Brown, Marcia Steele, Juanell Teague, Ms. "Marti", Jonathan Sprinkles, Delatorro McNeal II, Simon Bailey, Larry Winget, Albert and Tanya Mensah, Otis Williams, Keith Harrell, W Mitchell, Susan Levin, Rene Godefroy, Zig and Jean Ziglar. John, Karen and her Royal Highness Lindsay Alston, thank you for the most wonderful foreword.

To my spiritual leader, teacher and guide — the Honorable Bishop Kenneth C. Ulmer and First Lady Togetta Ulmer for being the noblest examples to our "Family of Faith" — thanks for the many lessons and blessings.

To my book dream-team, Kathi Dunn and Associates for the awesome cover design; Ron "Hobie" Hobart for the interior design; Susan Kendrick and Graham Van Dixhorn for the back and flap copywriting; and my brilliant editors Robin Quinn and Jack Barnard (*Jack, thanks for being my great speaking and creative writing coach.*)

To The Boeing Company, Ping and May Long, Ahyoung Alison Moon-Park, Pete and Antoinette Sterling, Tony and Nkechi Akpati, Lori Angela Walker, Wally Luther, Albert "Doctor" Welcher, Bruce Bertea, John Halchak, Anita Nicoletti, Curtis and Dawn Davis, Byron Wood, James Albaugh, Mike Jimerson, Bill Bellows and Phil Condit—your support is appreciated.

To Westchester High School, Cal State Northridge, Lehigh University, Pepperdine University and Oxford University—for my formal education.

To The Taplins, The Baylarks, The Claibornes, The Jordans, The Armstrongs, The Bonds, The Bowers, The Bavarians, The Diops, The Stricklands, The Goodsons, The Solomons, The Duboses, The McNishes, The Thompsons, The Iyams, The Savages, The Bahams, The Lavergnes, Joseph and Nicole Phillips, Robert and Karen Cole, Margaret June Brown, Gigi Littlejohn-McGuire, Leroy Geter, Dr. William Franklin, Dr. Leslie Small, Dean Emeritus Dr. Rick Ratcliffe, Alpha Phi Alpha Fraternity, Inc., The New Leaders, Tim Story, Glen and Cathy McClure, Monica and Kendall Fuselier, Dr. Henry Odi, Dr. Peter Likins, E. Kenneth, Joy and Kosi Nwabueze—for all you do for others.

My special gratitude goes to Tara and Lucius Davis, Debra Armstrong, my beautiful wife Aloria, my magnificent children Stephanie, Ahsaan and Ahmir for all your contributions to the success of my vision.

SPECIAL PRAISE FROM ZIG ZIGLAR

"Tony, as the Redhead said, 'You are something else!' With your excitement about life, your commitment to what you are doing, and your bubby personality—I believe you're going to make a difference in the lives of a lot of people."

—**Zig Ziglar**, Motivational Teacher and
Bestselling Author of *See You at the Top*

Contents

FOREWORD

Imagine that you had a penny for each person who ever said, *"If I had known then what I know now!"* You'd be among the wealthiest people on Earth! The truth is that there are things we all wish we had known before encountering certain events, conditions, or people in the past. In addition, many—if not most of us—move through life hoping and dreaming to accomplish things very quickly that will bring contentment and peace of mind. Yet the entire issue in living well has to do with learning to operate ourselves. This takes time. Tony Magee's *Can't Shove a Great Life into a Small Dream* is about learning to operate yourself more effectively.

Life is that period of time you have between birth and death. What you ultimately accomplish during your life depends on your awareness. And your awareness affects your decisions. Early awareness means being informed about things in a timely way. When you have the right knowledge when you need it, you can avoid loss, and grief, and prosper as you grow.

Can't Shove a Great Life into a Small Dream provides an opportunity to expand your awareness in a world where it is impossible to know everything. This book is a great jump-start because all you need at any given instant is to just know enough. And when you make it a habit to balance what you know with experience and insight, you will be prepared for what life demands and the unexpected events that reality often throws onto our paths.

This book will assist you in minimizing the negative impact of challenges, and at the same time, it will inspire you to persevere in a universe of unlimited possibilities. Herein you'll find a roadmap, reminders, and tools for success. For as you search for ways to live meaningfully, you'll find that the lack of awareness is the only thing that can imprison you.

In offering twelve life-changing principles for a lifetime of peace and progress—enhanced with a grandmother's wit and insight from many other sources—Tony Magee provides universal tools for you to fulfill your "meant to be." You will live more meaningfully when you enhance your growth with what is contained herein. *Can't Shove a Great Life into a Small Dream* can minimize moments of being disillusioned and confused—those instances that compel us to say, "I wish I had known then what I know now!"

John W. Alston, MS, CSP, CPAE
Co-Author of *Stuff Happens!*
Los Angeles, California

Introduction

"Your life is much more important than you could imagine. It is your first treasure."

—Dr. Maya Angelou

Imagine living the life that you have always wanted — having the hot career, the great relationship, and even a large bank account. *Can't Shove a Great Life into a Small Dream*™ provides you with a lifetime guide to overcome any obstacle between you and your dream—mainly your own self-limiting belief system—and to rediscover your untapped passion.

Allow me to ask you a simple question: What is the most important thing in this world for a human being? I've asked this question of dozens of friends and associates. Their answers run the gamut, but hardly anyone comes up with the word *"freedom."*

In America, we regularly read in newspapers and hear on the evening news examples of people who come to the United States without speaking a lick of English, with hardly any money to their name, and in a relatively short time, they rise to wonderful success.

For instance, Nido Qubein, a native of Lebanon, was seventeen years old when he came to America on his own with roughly fifty dollars in his pocket and not a single contact. He spoke no English. Today, Nido is chairman of an international consulting firm, as well as the owner of the Great Harvest Bread Company with 175 stores in thirty-four states across the U.S., and he serves on the executive board of a Fortune 500 financial corporation with over $70 billion in assets. He has written a number of best-selling books and is one of the hottest professional speakers in the world, addressing over a hundred business and professional groups every year. Over the years, Nido has become a multimillionaire and now he teaches others how to become the same.

Here's another example. One of my best friends from college, E. Kenneth Nwabueze, came to the United States from

Nigeria, West Africa in the pursuit of an American college education in the field of engineering. At first, he started at Pierce, a local community college located in Southern California's San Fernando Valley. After finishing at Pierce, Ken transferred to the local university, Cal State Northridge. This is where we met in the early 1990s. To earn money while attending engineering school, Ken started a business and built customized personal computers, selling them to students on campus and to local small businesses. This small but profitable business would eventually grow into SageMetrics™ Corporation, a $100 million Internet data-mining company with offices in Los Angeles and London. Post September 11th, 2001, Ken was appointed by President George W. Bush to serve as an advisor to the Department of Homeland Security. Today, he is a renowned science and technology consultant to world leaders.

Many people who move to the U.S. in search of fulfilling their dreams, typically achieve them at a much faster rate than those who were born and raised in America. Why? I believe it's because freedom is precious to those who never had it and want to experience a better way of life. As Americans, many of us basically take our freedom for granted. Feeling secure in our freedom and unmotivated, we often fail to achieve our dreams.

As an American child, I was born to a single mom caring for two teenage kids. My mother had to drop out of high school in the eleventh grade due to certain hardships. She raised us amid the poverty and violence at the hardened Nickerson Gardens Housing Projects in the Watts neighborhood of Los Angeles. Facing these harsh conditions, what would the future hold for Tony Magee?

My mother once told me that I might've been born into poverty, but poverty was not born in me. She said that I was her son, a child of God, and that I was made out of some very special ingredients. My mom told me that I was special—that I was bold, beautiful, black, and brilliant. At an early age, she convinced me that it was possible to obtain anything my eyes could see. She said, *"Son, all it takes is hope and a good plan."* All I ever wanted was a better life than the one I had inherited.

Surviving a very painful childhood and overcoming the enormous odds that were up against me, I was determined to escape. In my mind, I felt like Dorothy from the Wizard of Oz, when she sang, *"If itty-bitty birds can fly high over the rainbow —then why can't I?"* I figured that somehow I just needed to develop my wings.

December 17, 1986 was a day that changed my life forever. On this exciting day, I took my SAT exam to become one of the first in my family to go college. This would be a dream come true for everyone involved—especially my mother. On that same day, my mother—my earth who gave me life and many tidbits of wisdom unexpectedly died of heart failure. I was just sixteen years old and devastated. What was I to do now? I realized that I had a choice—was I going to become another negative ghetto statistic and succumb to the unstable situation that surrounded me or was I going to raise myself up out of the mud of my wretched environment? Well, I didn't want to be stuck in the mud.

You might wonder how I managed to move upward. *Tony, how did you go from the poverty and violence of the Nickerson Gardens Housing Projects in Watts to one day become an international scholar in business at Oxford University?* Looking back, I can see that the odds were against me. However, when I learned about my mother's death, I realized that I had to keep on going—that I could not enjoy the great life I wanted so badly with a small dream. I would need to learn the *Life-Essentials* that would make my dream possible. My basic goal was to make my mama proud of me. I just wanted to make her smile up in Heaven and say, *"now that's my baby right there."*

Today, when I think of my mother, one of the things that come to my mind is the engraving on her tombstone. It simply reads:

Novel Jean Taplin-Magee
May 18, 1938—December 17, 1986

The first date is the day she entered into this world. The second date is the day she exited. The three children that she had nurtured, the many lives that she touched, and all of the wonderful memories that she created for us are all summarized by one hyphen between those two dates. Everything my mother ever accomplished—or didn't—is now simply an unassuming little dash. It seems that when it's all said and done, life ends up being that tiny little dash between two dates engraved on a tombstone, and that tombstone sits on a graveyard plot that hardly anyone ever stops to visit.

What can you do to make your life an awesome life? What can you do to make your dash an awesome dash? Life just may be a little dash between your birth date and your death date, but you want to experience the best life possible—right? *Right!* The best thing you can do is to reduce your problems, prepare yourself for the unforeseen, enjoy the good times, endure the bad times, and then handle whatever is expected.

As you move through *Can't Shove a Great Life into a Small Dream*, you'll work through the *Twelve Life-Essentials*.

Life-Essential 1: *Being Inspired for an Education*—In the first chapter you'll see that we acquire the skills of living successfully through knowledge. Knowledge when properly applied equals power—it is fundamental. If you think education is too expensive, then try ignorance!

Life-Essential 2: *Defining Your Major Purpose in Life*—In Chapter Two you'll ask yourself, "What on Earth am I here for?" You'll learn the importance of finding and fulfilling your life's assignment. Your life purpose is directly linked to your true happiness.

Life-Essential 3: *Developing Self-Esteem*—I'll show you how to raise your level of self-worth, self-respect, and self-confidence in Chapter Three. Self-esteem is the single most important quality of highly successful people. You'll see that all of what we know is not nearly as important as how we feel about ourselves!

Life-Essential 4: *Navigating through Life's Changes*—The life-essential of Chapter Four will help you to embrace change versus fighting it. The only thing in life that's permanent is change.

Life-Essential 5: *Choosing A Positive Attitude*—You are what you think about all day long. We have the power to choose whether today is going to be a good day or a lousy one. I'll show you why your attitude is your most valuable possession in Chapter Five.

Life-Essential 6: *Setting Goals & Achieving Them*—The truth is that most of us don't have a problem achieving our goals; we have a problem setting them. Thus, you'll discover the importance of setting goals in order to achieve your dreams in Chapter Six.

Life-Essential 7: *Having Financial Discipline*—In Chapter Seven, you'll learn that money is not the root of all evil—the lack of money is. All dreams have to be financed in some way. It's money that makes the world go 'round. A dream without money to back it will never become a reality.

Life-Essential 8: *Becoming a Competent Leader*—In this chapter, you'll learn the traits of a leader and why clarity of vision for your dream is key.

Life-Essential 9: *Influencing the World around You*—In Chapter Nine, you'll master the art of persuasion and come to understand why you should see yourself as a brand to be marketed to the world. No matter who you are, your talents are absolutely marketable.

Life-Essential 10: *Creating Balance in Life*—This chapter presents simple ways to enjoy your life while making a living—to live for your passion and not your pension. You will learn to develop a style of living that creates balance and a sense of well-being in order to support who you are and where you are in every area of your life.

Life-Essential 11: *It Takes a Team to Fulfill a Dream*—Is your life filled with diverse people who are committed to a common goal? You can't rise above mediocrity without learning how to use the minds of other people. This chapter's life-essential will demonstrate why fulfilling your dreams is not a project for one person.

Life-Essential 12: *Great Readers Make Greater Leaders*—The last chapter offers my personal book list. Contained within this list may rest the unseen key, which when turned will unleash the power within you so you can live your dreams.

Thank you for the opportunity to share these profound strategies; they can deeply enhance the quality of your life!

They've been the secrets to my success both personally and professionally. I suggest that you read the contents of *Can't Shove a Great Life into a Small Dream* as though you and I are personal friends and I'm writing to you and only you.

For this program to achieve its maximum impact, I also recommend that you work through all of these Life-Essentials in sequence. There is logic to their order. Nevertheless, if you jump around or focus on only a couple of the strategies, they will still work. As you read, highlight the many new ideas, sentences, passages, and quotations that are meaningful to you. Keep this in mind: the sole purpose of this book is to inspire you to maximize your human potential and challenge you to live your best life!

You, too, can convert your natural talent, personality, creative thinking, knowledge, and energy into enormous success and happiness. *Can't Shove a Great Life into a Small Dream* tells you how, and if you let it, my book will inspire you to new heights never imagined! Your job is to look for the message in it that applies to you. When you recognize it, pay close attention and shift into action!

As you move through each of these twelve Life-Essentials of highly successful people, answering the questions at the end of each chapter will direct your mind into desired pathways. These questions were designed to help you tap into the immense potential you already possess.

As I coach business professionals, entrepreneurs, students, educators, entertainers, corporations, non profit organizations, and others, I am humbled by the power of these very common sense values to transform chaos into action and self-doubt into clarity. *Can't Shove a Great Life into a Small Dream* is like a *Thomas Guide* that will lead you peacefully and powerfully through unexplored personal paths.

Are you ready to transform your dreams into extraordinary greatness? I know you are—so let's go!

LIFE-ESSENTIAL  1

LIGHT AS A PEN, HEAVY AS A SPADE
Being Inspired for an Education

"If you think education is expensive, then try ignorance."
—Anonymous

In the game of life, knowledge is king. Only with knowledge can we learn how to live successfully, only with knowledge can we unleash the power that lies within all of us. Knowledge is king, and we enter the castle—the realm of royalty—when we consciously seek out the knowledge to change our lives.

The level of a person's knowledge and maturity will always determine his or her place in the world. All people are born ignorant and must, for a while, live in ignorance. But remember this: Those people who remain ignorant have only themselves to blame.

Today in our world, anyone who has not mastered the three Rs (reading, writing, and arithmetic) is likely to be found in the lowest level of our stratified social mass. To fully grasp this concept, it's helpful to picture the structure of our society in the form of a pyramid. The base is a broad square, with each of the four corners gradually rising inward to a high central point. Sadly, the great majority of people are to be found within the large bottom portion of this pyramid. The higher you ascend, the smaller the stratums. At the very top of the pyramid dwell the most magnificent people on Earth.

Many of us may not be naturally outfitted to reach the zenith. However, each person does have control over where they will live between the highest peak and the lowest level. "Not having" is no excuse for "not getting." The legendary Blues singer Billie Holiday said it best when she sang, *"Mama may have... Papa may have... but God bless the child that got his own... that got his own."*

Keep in mind that the higher you go up on a pyramid, the farther you can see, the cleaner and crisper the air is to breathe, and the less crowded it becomes. Furthermore, the greatest incentive while rising up the pyramid is that as we climb, we help most of those around us to do the same.

A Grandmother's Wit

In my elementary school years, my mother would often allow me to stay with my grandmother during extended school holidays and summer vacations. At that time, "Mama"—that's what everyone (family and friends of the family) called my grandmother—lived in Stevenson Village, a Los Angeles suburb in Carson, California. Carson is just southwest of Compton and Watts. I loved to go stay at Mama's house. Her neighborhood was a safe community for children to play in, plus Mama lived on a cul-de-sac. The best part was that Mama would let me and my cousins eat as many peanut butter and jelly sandwiches as we wanted, and everyday she would buy one pack of Now & Later candies from the ice-cream man, for all of us to share. Also, Mama made the very best hot-water cornbread and southern fried chicken in the world!

I had lots and lots of friends in Carson. I remember how we used to play red-light-green-light, hide-and-go-seek, and flag football. We would also ride our bikes and skate all around the neighborhood in those familiar blue skates with the red and white stripes we all got for Christmas (every year). My playmates and I were much like "The Little Rascals." We would play outside all day long—sometimes up to ten hours.

My grandmother, Mattie Marie Taplin, loved to tell us stories of her childhood, about growing up on Big Daddy's farm in Clarksdale, Mississippi. Big Daddy or Papa, as she would affectionately call him, was Mama's father.

Mama would talk about how hard life was back on Big Daddy's farm. She told us tales of how she and her siblings had to walk 150 miles to school, over a gigantic hill, in the snow with no shoes. Then 150 miles back home just to help Big Daddy on his farm. No matter how fantastic the stories were she always made her point. There was constantly work to be done. She said that in the summertime, they would work on Papa's farm from *"can't see in the morning until can't see at night"*—plowing the fields, picking vegetables and cotton, and milking those cows. They even made their own ice cream out of fresh snow.

Mama also noticed just how much time we kids spent playing foolish games, running around outdoors, and some of the mischief we got into around the neighborhood. She often discouraged me from wanting to play so much with my little knuckle-headed friends.

I remember one particularly hot summer day in 1978, when it felt like the inside of an oven on the streets in Carson. I was nine years old at the time. My team was up by two touchdowns and Jimmy passed me the pigskin. I ran as fast as I could—darting left, then faking right, as I headed for the end zone. I was Tony Dorsett—flying in the wind—scoring another spectacular touchdown. Suddenly the air was filled with the sound of "TONNNNNNY!!!" I froze in my tracks. I knew that sound all-too-well so I hollered back, "Yes Ma'am, Mama!" She said, "Come home right this minute, I have some work for you to do." All my friends were upset, mumbling, "Man Tony, you gotta go? We're not finish playin' our game yet. How come yo' grandmother always callin' you when we're having fun? Why you gotta go now, Man? Man, yo' grandmamma sure is mean."

I said to them, "Yeah man, but if I don't go, she might whoop me with her Mississippi strap. I don't want my five-foot-two behind whooped by a woman who's four-foot-nine. Man, I gotta go—see y'all later."

I knew that if I didn't respond with a quickness, Mama's

call would be followed by that strap across my backside. And believe me, I didn't want any part of that 'cause my grandmother knew how to whip!

After I got to the house, we headed for the backyard. Mama asked me to dig a hole for her new rose bush. That July day, it was hotter than all of Africa, two Indias and a Victorville. Mama said to me, "Baby, I want you to take that there spade (a shovel) and dig Mama a hole for this here rose bush." Using her hands to emphasize the dimensions, she said, "Dig Mama a hole this big-a-round and this-here deep." Mama instructed me to dig the hole near an old brick-walled fence away from the vegetable garden where her turnips, collards, and mustard greens were usually planted.

As my face dripped with dirty-salty sweat, I took the spade and began digging the hole. Mama went back inside the house, saying that she would come out soon to check on me. As my mind drifted, the sweat began to drench my clothes and the inside of my mouth started to taste like I had just sucked on a dozen lemons. I thought I smelled... Mama's good ol' southern fried chicken and hot water cornbread! Then I thought... *I'd give anything right now for a plate, but instead I have to dig this stupid hole.* The time passed so slowly that each beat of my heart seemed like an eternity.

Thirty minutes went by, then an hour, then an hour and fifteen minutes. An eternity of eternities. I had not gotten even two inches beneath the top surface of the soil! Frustrated and thirsty, I started getting mad at the dirt. I even kicked it a few times. I couldn't believe that I was missing football to dig a hole in the ground. Finally, Mama returned to the backyard with a pitcher of ice-cold lemonade and two large jelly-jar glasses. She said, "You ain't finished diggin' Mama's hole yet, Baby? What's taking you so long?" I told her, "Mama, this dirt is harder than steel."

Mama told me to take a break and have a glass of lemonade with her. I was happy 'cause it was burnin' hot outside and plus Mama made a special kind of lemonade. It would be so good and sugar-sweet that you'd have to take your shoes off so you could wiggle your toes—it was that Mississippi stuff! I gulped down my first two glasses in less than a minute. After wiping my face and mouth with my dirty shirt, I told Mama,

"Sorry I couldn't dig that hole for you. I tried, Mama. I even have blisters on my hands to prove it."

Mama's voice was filled with compassion as she told me that the reason I couldn't dig a hole in this particular area was because there was a block of excess cement just beneath the surface of the dirt—from that old brick fence. She said, "Baby, on the surface, the ground by that there fence looks the same as the rest of the yard. But ain't it funny how folk always say *"what you don't know won't hurt you?"* I want you to know that *what you don't know can kill you.* You didn't know about that hidden chunk of concrete, now did you? Tell me again—how does those blisters on your hands feel?"

Mama knew all along what she was doing. I was upset, but knowing Mama—she had a reason for it all. She was teaching me about life and education. She continued, "Children now-a-days play entirely too much and think they know everything. What they need to know is the value of hard work, and what they need to do is spend more time preparing for their future. They need that "down home" kind of discipline. It takes a village to raise a lil' child, but if that village is crazy—then they'll raise some very crazy kids. Tony, you my grandchild and you gon' go to one of them great big ol' colleges some day and make something of yourself. Mama want you to have a better chance at livin' a good life for yourself—than the ones your lil' mannish friends gon' have when they get grown. I mean it, now! I'm serious child! You see... Mama didn't have all the wonderful opportunities that you young folk take for granted today."

As a working farm girl from Clarksdale, Mississippi, my grandmother was only able to finish the ninth grade. Not because she wasn't bright—in fact, she was one of the smartest pupils in all of her classes. Mama and her eleven brothers and sisters all had to lend their hands to labor Big Daddy's farm. She thought wisely to place an emphasis on the value of education for me.

In retrospect, this event has become the most important defining moment of my life. I often ask myself where I would have ended up without my grandmother's wisdom and her belief in my ultimate success.

Surviving the deprivation and hostility within the concrete-block walls of Watts Nickerson Gardens Housing

Projects where I lived with my mother—earning a Bachelor's Degree in Industrial Engineering; becoming the first African-American to receive a Master's degree in Material Science and Engineering from Lehigh University; obtaining an MBA from Pepperdine; completing Executive MBA studies at Oxford University in England and enjoying a quality life—it all turned out to be much easier than I imagined. The hardest thing was—believing that I could. My grandmother knew, and surely believed that I could.

As Mama would put it, the moral of the story is, *"Tony, with education, you'll get the best chance to live your best life. A good education will change the whole game, add letters to the back of your name, change your address and more importantly, change your bank account. Baby, with a really good education—your life's work will be as light as a pen; without it your life's work will be as heavy as that spade."*

Up Against the Odds: In Search for Excellence

Gang violence, juvenile delinquency, academic underachieve-ment, low teacher expectation, and high school drop-outs are a few of the areas I challenged by earning higher degrees of educa-tion. More importantly, each area has been an intricate part of my personal experience.

As an African-American man-child growing up in South Central Los Angeles, my encounter with these perils was life-threatening at times, yet vital as it relates to my many aspirations. My interest in pursuing a career in Science and Engineering, plus Business Administration, was motivated by the adversity, despair, and dysfunction that I have been fortu-nate enough to experience and transcend.

My quest for personal and professional excellence required three fundamental, life-giving elements in order to succeed: (1) being my own authority (self-driven), (2) believing in myself (faith), (3) exercising my creative mind. I call them *Tony's ABC's. A: Authority; B: Belief; C: Creativity.*

Authority... You Must be Self-Driven in Your Life

This value insists that, as a human being, you rely on God and yourself—not the outside world to get your life together. This value depends on looking in the mirror and truthfully assessing your gifts and shortcomings. To truly be at the top of the game takes both practice and commitment. Having *authority* in your life compels you to dip into your deepest awareness, regain your lost memory and shape your world accordingly. You have a special truth to bring to the world. Only when you have authority in your life can you recapture your gifts and talents and effectively, dynamically share them with the rest of us. Only when you let go of needing other people to ratify, verify, and certify your existence can you uniquely reflect your capacity for human greatness and progress.

In fact, the first act of a free person is to shape the world in his or her own interest and likeness. Intrinsically, this act is a testimony to both the acceptance of self and the commitment to one's own authority. Franz Fanon, author of *Wretched of the Earth*, teaches us that we must ask ourselves three basis questions. These essential questions are: *"Who am I?" "Am I really who I am?"* And, *"Am I all I ought to be?"* The answers to these questions will reflect a person's culture and history as well as personal identity. We must remain aware of our power to shape a strong personal identity and grow a positive future, despite any negative influences of our past.

Belief… You Have Faith in Yourself and in Your World

The second value is *Belief*. Belief is an act of faith, a deep confidence in and commitment to all that we hold near and dear: ourselves, our families, our businesses, our communities, the culture at large. Humans evolve through belief. Only when we believe deeply in ourselves and in the possibility for our fellow humans to live righteously and responsibly, do we approach the potential of our incarnation. In times such as these, belief is often blind. Certain members within our society would try to convince us that humans are no better than animals—not to be trusted, not worthy of our time and attention.

Belief—first in self—then in all others is an act of deep compassion and timeless wisdom.

Having faith in ourselves is key. Two words that should be considered by everyone as self-defining acronyms are "fear" and "faith." F.E.A.R. is False Evidence Appearing Real, while F.A.I.T.H. is Finding Answers In The Heart.

Leading psychologists suggest that there are only two innate fears in a human being. They say that we are all born with fear of falling and of loud noise. *Every other fear is learned thereafter.* For example, a person might have a fear of rats, going to the dentist, or speaking in public settings. To be honest with you, these were personal fears of mine that took me a while to conquer. Nevertheless, I did it. I handled those fears as one would an enemy.

"Without faith, nothing is possible. With it, nothing is impossible."
—Mary Mcleod Bethune

Overcoming Fear

As I mentioned above, going to the dentist was a big psychological problem for me. I come from a family of "dental chickens." With rare exception, I can't recall anyone in my family going to the dentist every six months for regular checkups. Instead of going to prevent dental caries from occurring, most of my relatives would only visit the dentist's office if they needed some major work done—like getting a tooth pulled. Why? While money was an issue, it was mostly because of fear. For example, my mom was very afraid of going to the dentist. I learned my fear from her. If it was too scary for my mama, then it was too scary for me too—because I loved my mama. The fear within my family either originated from some painful personal experiences or it was simply passed down through the generations.

As a young adult, I realized that if I didn't risk change and overcome this fear of dental work, I was going to end up with a "yuck mouth" smile like a whole lot of older people that I knew. In my heart, I wanted to break out of this perpetual cycle of fear and give my future smile a chance. What I needed was a great dentist, one who was also a great psychologist. I needed someone who could rehabilitate dental chickens. Then I met a man named Greg Rubin, DDS. Through this wonderful dentist, I learned as William James once said, *"Your belief at the beginning of a doubtful undertaking is the one thing that insures the successful outcome of your venture."* With Dr. Rubin's help, I overcame my fear of dentistry and have excellent dental health today.

Here's how I overcame my fear. It was through these four basic steps:

Step 1 - I identified exactly what I feared the most.

Step 2 - I wrote down everything that could possibly go wrong if I did what I was afraid of.

Step 3 - I outlined specific ways to overcome my fear.

Step 4 - I used the V.I.P.E.R. methodology:

- *Verbalizing* my fear of visiting the dentist aloud.

- *Imagining* myself relaxing in Dr. Rubin's dentistry chair as he worked on my teeth.

- *Practicing* the whole event in my mind, thoroughly—with a positive mental attitude.

- *Experiencing* the whole process by breaking my fears into easier parts to handle.

- *Relaxing, relaxing, relaxing* through every step of the process.

As I was growing up, encountering fear was painful at times. Although I had a strong obsessive drive to succeed in life, simultaneously I was hindered by an equally strong self-doubt. Often I encountered feelings of meagerness and possessed perhaps the largest inferiority complex in the world (or at least this was my belief). I learned early on that others truly do appraise you at the level of your own self-respect, self-confidence, and self-image.

It has been said that self-knowledge is the dawn of wisdom. Often it is also the first phase of a remedy to abnormal fear. But, to remove fear, more is required. Chiefly, old fears must be replaced with something positive—a strong faith—otherwise, they will either recur or new fears will take their place.

"You gotta love yourself, Baby. You gotta love yourself so much that when you walk down the street—- you can smell the same kind of love on other people."

—Jill Scott

Creativity… *Exercising Your Creative Mind*

My father-in-law, the late Michael Moses Armstrong once told me a funny joke about this talented scientist who had challenged God to a creativity contest. *The scientist said to God, "God, I think that I can create anything that you can create—maybe even a bit better." Then God replied, "You do? Okay then, you bigheaded genius, this sounds like a challenge to me—I'm up for it." Then the scientist said to God, "Name anything and I bet I can make it—even better than you!" God smiled, "Okay little man, I'll make it easy on you—let's make a human being." God added, "But you have to make the human being out of dirt, just like I did in the beginning." So, the pompous scientist said, "No problem!" and kneeled down to collect some of the earth's dirt. And at that moment, God kindly taps him on his hand and says to him, "First you have to make your own dirt!"*

This last value is *Creativity*. Once you accept the idea that you—and not others around you—are the Authority in your life, and then understand that the world moves in the direction of your belief, then, like an artist, you are ready to paint the world a better picture. You are a creative being and your creativity—in all its manifest forms—is the key to fulfilling your own dreams and to making our planet the paradise it deserves to be. No matter what you do for a living, no matter what your interests, unearth your creativity and paint the sky the brightest colors in your palette.

When I think of creative genius, my hero George Washington Carver comes to mind. He is best known for his unparalleled work with the ordinary peanut. *It was told to me that Carver prayed to the Lord for all the wisdom in the universe. The Lord denied Carver, told him that he could not handle that much wisdom, and required him to pray for something more reasonable. So then Carver said… "Lord? Would you please grant me all the wisdom of this here PEANUT?" The Lord kindly said, "So be it!" and answered Carver's prayer.*

At the Tuskegee Institute in Alabama, George Washington Carver successfully developed his soil-enriching crop rotation method, which alternated nitrate-producing peanuts and peas with nitrate-depleting cotton. Following Brother Carver's lead, southern farmers soon began planting peanuts one year and cotton the next. Though many of the peanuts were used to feed livestock, large surpluses quickly developed. Carver then came up with 325 different uses for the extra peanuts—from cooking oil to printer's ink. When he discovered that the sweet potato and the pecan also enriched depleted soils, Carver found almost twenty uses for those crops, including synthetic rubber and material for paving highways.

You know, if it weren't for Mr. Carver, I couldn't have enjoyed all those peanut butter and jelly sandwiches as a little kid. With the knowledge of one tiny peanut, Carver successfully developed his crop rotation method, which saved the economy in the South and grew many new industries and opportunities.

"Anything will give up its secrets if you love it enough—ask and listen."

—George Washington Carver

"Be brave enough to live life creatively. The creative is the place where no one else has ever been. You have to leave the city of your comfort and go into the wilderness of your intuition. You can't get there by bus, only by hard work and risk and by not quite knowing what you're doing. What you'll discover will be wonderful. What you'll discover will be yourself."

—Alan Alda

All Advice Isn't Good Advice

While I was in the tenth grade, a high-school administrator told me that at the rate I was going, I would not amount to much. Now, at my current level of education and achievement, I can see that this was not the most appropriate thing to say to an "at-risk" fifteen year old. Instead of using it as a closing statement, her comment should have been the preface to a conversation about how I might define some attainable goals that could turn my situation around.

If I had known back then what I know now, I would have told her something like what Jill Scott, my favorite R&B singer and poet, wrote: *Lady "your background… it ain't squeaky clean; sometimes we all gotta swim upstream. You ain't no saint, we're all a sinner. But you put your good foot down and make your soul the winner!"*

In retrospect, I don't think the Administrator made her comment maliciously. Her assessment was based on an upper-middle-class worldview and on the adverse circumstances present in my poverty-stricken environment at that time.

Instead of conceding to the adversity or accepting her prophesy regarding my future, I reached deep inside and discovered a personal resolve, and constructive anger that had gone untapped. Those qualities have proven to be my inner fuel for continued resilience and success. That lady didn't know whom she was dealing with. I learned through this experience that someone else's opinion of me doesn't have to become my reality. William Goethe said, *"Look at a man the way that he is—he only becomes worse; but look at him as if he were what he could be—then he becomes what he should be."* You know, we have to thank God sometimes for those who believe in us when we don't even believe in ourselves. And you must practice self-love.

"When you judge another, you do not define them, you define yourself."

—Dr. Wayne Dyer

Remember When You Said I Wouldn't Ever Be Nuthin'?

One time in an interview, Muhammad Ali, the Heavyweight Boxing Champion, hit the nail on the head. Often people say some pretty harsh things that ultimately inspire us to great heights. In Muhammad Ali's case, these words came when he was twelve years old from a schoolteacher—a person who should have encouraged him

Ali recollects… "To one teacher, I was just another loudmouth. She came up to me one day and said, 'You ain't never gonna be nuthin'.' But I won the Golden Gloves in Louisville when I was seventeen, and the next year, I won the gold medal at the 1960 Rome Olympics. First thing I did when I got home was go straight to the teacher's classroom.

"'Remember when you said I wouldn't ever be nuthin'?' She looked surprised. 'I am the greatest in the world,' I said, holding my medal by the ribbon. That doubting schoolteacher gave me all the motivation I ever needed to become the greatest of all time."

"You may not realize it when it happens, but a kick in the teeth may be the best thing in the world for you."
—Walt Disney

Only One Secret to Success

I would like to share with you that there is only one secret to success and that is HARD WORK! And when you also employ the three factors I've just prescribed—*becoming self-driven, exercising your creative mind, and believing in yourself (faith)*, the onward and upward mobility of your life, your family, your respective organization, and your community will become a reality.

Les Brown, author of *Live Your Dreams* personally taught me that as a human being with unlimited potential, you have the POWER...

To touch a life...

To mold a future...

To constantly grow and learn...

To challenge yourselves... each day, every day...

To always make a difference...

For within your HEART and MIND lies the SPIRIT of GREATNESS...

Within you lies MAGIC!"

Now, to help discover your personal magic, complete the following exercise and then continue on to Life-Essential Two.

LIFE-ESSENTIAL ONE EXERCISE

1. Make out a want list. Write down everything that you would like to see come about in your life. Include ways of gaining higher knowledge.

2. After completing your list of wants, prioritize them.

3. List opportunities that surround you now in your current situation. Brainstorm; write down whatever comes to mind.

4. Assess whether you are working not only hard, but also intelligently.

5. Set goals for increasing your knowledge in your area of interest and for upgrading your personal and professional skills.

6. Write down the greatest fear that you have overcome.

7. Write a brief statement about how you overcame that fear. What did you do, how did you do it, and what feelings did you have afterward?

YOUR LIFE IS LIKE A MIST

Defining Your Major Purpose In Life

> "Whereas ye know not what shall be on the morrow. For what is your life? It is even a vapour, that appeareth for a little time, and vanisheth away."
>
> —James 4:14

Our Natural Desires Abandoned

As a child growing up in the 1970s, I used to watch a television show hosted by Lorne Greene titled *Lorne Greene's New Wilderness*. In one episode, which focused on the African elephant, I remember how strong and peaceful these creatures appeared in their natural habitat. I also recall seeing elephants like this performing tricks and stunts at the Ringling Bros. and Barnum & Bailey Circus. Wearing satin clothing with beautifully beaded head garments, the elephants would stand up on their hind legs and walk all around like human beings; then they would lie down and roll over like housedogs. Some even danced like John Travolta to the then-popular tune "Stayin' Alive" from the *Saturday Night Fever* sound track. While watching, I asked myself: *How in the world did they learn to do all this?*

With research, I discovered that there is much pain and suffering involved in the training of circus animals. In order to train an elephant in captivity, a strong chain is attached to the animal's ankle. The chain is then attached to a steel stake embedded in concrete. When the elephant learns that no amount of pulling will free him, he no longer tries. Once the elephant has learned this, the trainer replaces the heavy chain with a light cord. The elephant feels the cord, knows it is tethered, and does not pull against it—even though the cord could be easily broken!

What's the point of my story? Like circus elephants, you and I have been socialized and trained. In his book *Find Purpose Find Power*, Denton L. Roberts explains that our training has greatly influenced the development of our personalities. Our training teaches us that there are certain limits and parameters within which we must function—even if they stifle the expression of our truest desires!

Sadly we see the world the way we have been trained to see it and often abandon our natural desires. Unconsciously, we have created a paradigm of reality based on certain beliefs about the world and ourselves. These beliefs become our worldview and shape our decisions and judgments. Consequently, our decisions and judgments may or may not encourage the development of our original self.

"If one advances confidently in the direction of his dreams to live the life he has imagined, he will meet with a success unexpected in common hours."
—Henry David Thoreau

A Ship Without a Captain

Successful living requires that you devote yourself to fulfilling a worthy life plan. If you don't consciously commit yourself to giving your life purpose and direction, you will be like a ship without a captain; this kind of vessel is destined to end up shipwrecked on *Gilligan's Island*.

Earl Nightingale, the late multifaceted author and Hall of Fame broadcasting personality, said, *"It is estimated that about 95 percent of people can be compared to ships without rudders. Subject to every shift of wind and tide, they're helplessly adrift. And while they fondly hope that they will one-day drift into some rich and exciting port, you and I know that for every narrow harbor entrance, there are a thousand miles of rocky coastline. The chances of their drifting into port are a thousand and one against them."*

"Make the most of yourself, for that is all there is of you."
—Ralph Waldo Emerson

Are You a Sheep-Lion?

An old fable comes to my mind about a pregnant lioness in the African jungle. The lioness spotted a group of lambs and decided to get one for her supper. As she went to attack, she gave birth to a cub and died right there on the spot!

The lambs took the baby lion and raised it. Eventually, the lion started to eat grass like a lamb. He bleated and cried like a lamb. Even as the cub grew bigger and stronger, he had this lamb mentality. The lion thought he too was a lamb!

One day, another lion came trotting by. When he looked over at this group of sheep, there was this big ol' lion acting like a lamb! The sheep-lion was eating grass and crying like a lamb. The second lion wanted to go talk to his "brother" to try to wake him up. But when the sheep saw the second lion coming, they ran—and so did the sheep-lion. He didn't even recognize his brother. The second lion was patient though and thought, "Nah, I just can't turn my back on my brother...I've got to try and help him."

A few days later, while the sheep were asleep, the second lion crept into the little group of animals. He tapped the sheep-lion on the shoulder and whispered kindly, "listen brother, you're a lion!" The sheep-lion answered, "No way man, I'm not a lion. I'm a sheep." The second lion replied, "Look, just come with me," and although he was more than a little suspicious, the sheep-lion followed.

The lion took the sheep-lion to a pond and said, "Now look into the water." When you see your reflection, it will be just like mine." The sheep-lion looked and said, "You're right!" The second lion continued: "Now, I want you to do something else. I want you to roar like this." The lion stuck his chest out and he ROARED! The sheep-lion tried—"Naaaaeeeellllll!!"—but it just wouldn't come out right. The sheep-lion's new buddy said, "Don't give up, you can do this." So finally the sheep-lion mustered up all of his strength and let out a mighty ROAR-RRRRRRRRR like a lion!

That was the convincer. He knew he was a sheep no more. He was indeed a lion.

What is the pond that helps us define who you are and reflects your major purpose in life?

"When you are inspired by some great purpose, some extraordinary project, all your thoughts break their bonds; your mind transcends limitation, your consciousness expands in every direction, and you find yourself in a new great and wonderful world. Dormant forces, faculties and talents become alive and you discover yourself to be a greater person by far than you ever dreamed."
—Patanjali

Living Well Cannot Be an Accident

Living well is not an accident. Your life must be on purpose; you must intend to do what you do. For instance, you must intend to be happy. If you don't intend to be happy, happiness will escape you. Happiness requires work. You have to work at it. You have to try to be happy.

Sometimes you need to reorganize your priorities in order to be happy. And certain things that make you unhappy should not be thought about. Why beat yourself up thinking about those things? We must think ourselves into happiness.

Yes, living well will never happen by accident. A good marriage doesn't happen by accident. Good kids do not happen by accident. A good day doesn't happen by accident. You choose to make it a good day. It is totally up to you!

"Your destiny is not a matter of chance—it is a matter of choice. Many people have the right aims in life—they just never get around to pulling the trigger."
—John Mason

A Sense of Mission

Dr. Wayne Dyer, author of the best-selling book How to Be a No-Limit Person, states that we spend most of our days learning and living by the rules and behaviors society has adopted and taught us. Much of this is valuable, but these rules don't lead us to a sense of personal mission in life.

To have a sense of individual purpose we must look to a different set of rules. A large part of this requires listening to your inner signals. This might also be thought of as "having your own mind." To allow another individual or group to control your mind in any way makes you a prisoner by your own decree. This is critical because your thoughts become the blueprints, which attract from your subconscious mind all the elements that go into fulfilling your concepts, whether positive or negative. What you have in your life right now is the outward manifestation of what has been going on in your mind. You have literally attracted everything that has come into your life—good or bad, happy or sad, successful or not. And this includes all facets of experience, be it business, marriage, health, or personal affairs.

"The purpose of life is to discover your gift. The meaning of life is giving your gift away."
—David Viscott

What's Your Life Assignment?

You must live your life truthfully. The reality of Truth is that you are here on divine assignment. It is important to understand that the Creator has planted you here on purpose. There is not a single person on Earth who arrived by accident. Nothing in existence is by accident, but by providence. The Creator has lovingly and patiently navigated every step of your life to bring you to where you are presently. In this way, you can now move further along on your journey to become all that you were created for. Your purpose is to fulfill God's purpose, and you do that by completing your life assignment.

In thinking about your personal assignment consider the following story of one of the most effective spiritual leaders on the scene today.

Bishop Kenneth C. Ulmer, author of *Spiritually Fit to Run the Race*, was an undergraduate at the University of Illinois. One semester he signed up for a course in criminology entitled "The Sociology of Criminals." To this day, Ulmer doesn't know why he took this class, but he did.

Ulmer went into the class the first night and got the syllabus with all of the assignments for the semester. It was the type of class that had a paper and a final project. His overall grade would be based on only one or two papers and the project. So Ulmer only went to the class the first couple of nights. Weeks later he noticed on the syllabus that there was a mid-term paper due in a few days. As usual, he had waited until the last minute, being the "Mr. Procrastinator" that he was.

To prepare the paper, Ulmer went to the library day and night. He crammed and studied, studied and crammed. Ulmer looked at research periodicals, books, footnotes, file-cards and everything else related. Then he went back to the class at the mid-term to hand in his paper. Ulmer was just so proud of himself. He had worked so hard on this paper.

Kenneth Ulmer came back to class the next week and the instructor passed out the graded papers. When Ulmer got his back, he noticed that the teacher had written some notes on the paper. At the top of the cover page a note read: GREAT PAPER. Good Research. Grade… F.

This wasn't a casual F. It was the kind of F that is written in bright red ink with a great-big circle around it. It seemed to Ulmer at the time that it really didn't take all of that to make the instructor's point. He felt a smaller F written in black ink would have been sufficient.

Then Ulmer noticed that his professor had written another note at the bottom of the paper. It said: "Great paper Kenny, but this was not the assignment!"

Ulmer had spent hours and hours—cramming and studying. He had been so proud of himself when he turned the paper in, despite his negligence at the beginning of the semester. He felt that he had caught up and had done a great job. In fact, he did do a great job, but it was the wrong job!

Oh what a tragedy it would be to stand before the Creator at the Kingdom of Heaven, with the memory of all your accomplishments and the accompanying accolades, only to hear God say, "Great life, but that was not your assignment."

"Many people work hard to climb the ladder of success, and suddenly find that their ladder is leaning up against the wrong wall."
—Don Hutson, Co-Author of *The Contented Achiever*

Finding Your Purpose Is Like Going Shopping

It takes a while for many people to find their purpose in life. One gauge we can use to help us is our talent. If you are multi-talented, it will take maturity to weigh out your stronger talents. Once this is accomplished, you should stimulate those one or two strong talents and determine where they fit in the bigger picture for your life. Some rare folks—like Jennifer "J-Lo" Lopez—manage to vacillate between many talents. She's an actor, singer, fashion designer, and restaurateur. But this is not the best course for most of us.

What application is best suited for your talents? For example, a singer may have some of the same skills as an actor or comedian. An actor and a trial attorney may have similar skills. A trial attorney may also be a brilliant writer like John Grisham, best- selling author of *The Firm, The Pelican Brief* and *The Rainmaker.*

Unfortunately, many people spend their days living in the vicinity of their purpose. But what gets massive life results is when you specifically define it. Finding one's purpose in life is just like what a woman goes through when she's out shopping for that special dress. She's looking for something special, but she doesn't know exactly what. She knows roughly what size to buy, but she still has to try the dress on to see if it fits. Then she has to look at it to decide if the dress is the right color, the right style, and whether or not it fits the occasion. But guess what? When the dress is right, it's REALLY RIGHT!

This is similar to determining your life purpose. No one can tell you exactly what your purpose should be, but I can tell you this—when it's right, it's REALLY RIGHT! Take time to assess your stronger talents. Then exercise them to see where they fit in the bigger picture. Once you try them out in the world, you'll see your true purpose shining through and know it is the right thing.

Definiteness of Purpose

Napoleon Hill, author of *Think and Grow Rich*, was one of the first people to teach that the science of personal achievement requires a definiteness of purpose. To reach that point can be a journey in itself. In his famous book, Hill writes that in order to realize your life purpose, you may need to break through blocks like fear, arrogance, ill health, poverty, or addictions. Only then may your soul genuinely express itself and serve the world.

Fortunately, as your life naturally unfolds, you will go through many different activities that offer a variety of ways to consider your overall purpose. Along the way, you will apply your personality skills and talents—such as communication, organization, care-giving, leadership, meditation, writing, designing, or public speaking. And as your life progresses, you may find yourself serving in more expansive and inclusive ways, as your soul takes a stronger and more prominent role in guiding the conduct of your life.

"Be patient toward all that is unsolved in your heart and try to love the questions themselves. Do not now seek the answers, which cannot be given you because you would not be able to live them and the point is to live everything. Live the questions now. Perhaps you will then gradually, without noticing it, live along some distant day into the answer."
—Rainer Maria Rilke

Now, to help you define your major purpose, complete the following exercises and then read on.

LIFE-ESSENTIAL TWO EXERCISE
Part One

You can begin defining your major purpose in life by completing the following:

1. As a young child (between the ages of five and eight years of age) what did you mainly get criticized for? You are bound to discover that your life purpose is directly linked to the subject of this criticism.

2. If you only had one more year to live, what things would be important to you?

3. Applying what you just learned above about your values, what can you see that should be a part of your life today—and perhaps every day?

4. If you were to describe "the life you have imagined" for yourself, what would it look like?

5. Are you living this life now? If not, why not?

6. As you look back over your life, what does your purpose appear to be?

7. To fulfill your purpose, as you understand it, you still need to:

Part Two

Once your purpose is clarified, do the following ten things:

1. Write out a clear statement of your major purpose in life. Sign it and then commit the statement to memory. Repeat your purpose statement at least twice daily in the form of a prayer or affirmation.

2. Create a clear outline of the plan or plans you intend to use to achieve the object of your definite major purpose.

3. State the maximum of time you'll allow to achieve it.

4. Describe in detail precisely what you intend to give in return for the realization of the object of your purpose. (Keep this in mind: everything has a just price, which must be paid.)

5. Keep your definite major purpose to yourself. (There are dream killers out there.)

6. Call your purpose into your conscious mind as often as may be practical.

7. Eat and sleep with it.

8. Take it with you every hour of the day.

9. Go the extra mile when working toward accomplishing your goals. It always pays.

10. And lastly, don't drift through life without aim or purpose. We all must have purpose.

LIFE-ESSENTIAL 3

CHURNIN' MILK INTO BUTTER
Developing Self-Esteem

*"If you love yourself, only then can you give love away. How can
you give what you don't feel?"*
—An Old Proverb

Bananas Are Brown Too!

I remember an experience I had when I was in the first grade at
Saint Paul Lutheran School in Lynwood, California. My teacher,
Mrs. Pierce, had instructed our class to use our brand-new
crayons to color a particular fruit on an assigned worksheet.
There were five different kinds of fruit to color. Pupils had strawberries, apples, oranges, grapes or bananas. The picture on my
worksheet was of a bunch of bananas. I was excited about this
assignment. Coloring in the first grade was my favorite activity. I
was a great coloring artist. I was the Master of the Crayon!

When we all finished coloring our fruit, Mrs. Pierce had a
"show and tell." First, she called upon Melissa to display her
beautiful red strawberries. Then, Mark got up and showed us his
orange oranges. Next, Howard stood up with his purple grapes.
Mrs. Pierce had gone through the whole class roster before she

called me up to her desk for my show and tell. With a big smile on my face, I held up my picture of bananas before the class. There was a pause and then everyone began to laugh out loud. Mrs. Pierce was laughing even louder than the other students. I didn't understand, so I asked my teacher, "What is so funny and why is everybody laughing at me?" She replied, "How silly of you to color your bananas brown. Everyone knows that bananas are yellow."

I was devastated and began to cry. Now Mrs. Pierce was the one who couldn't understand: why was I so upset? You see, when bananas are freshly picked for produce, they are usually light green. When they are distributed, they are first delivered to the more affluent communities in shades between light green and faint yellow. But by time those same bananas made it to various parts of my community within South-Central Los Angeles, they were a dull yellow with big brown spots. And when they finally got to my house, those same bananas were brown. At the age of six, this was what I knew. Brown bananas were my reality while attending the privileged Saint Paul Lutheran School. *Mrs. Pierce, I did successfully complete your assignment. Bananas are brown too!*

"If I care to listen to every criticism, let alone act on them, then this shop may as well be closed for all other businesses. I have learned to do my best, and if the end result is good, then I do not care for any criticism, but if the end result is not good, then even the praise of ten angels would not make the difference."
—Abraham Lincoln

The Key to Failure or Success

Self-esteem is the single most important quality of highly successful people. It is that deep-down feeling of one's own self-worth, self-respect, and self-confidence.

As you look around at your fellow human beings, you will find it hard to ignore the fact that very few people are happy and fulfilled or leading purposeful lives. Why is that? Most of them seem to be merely coping with their problems and the circumstances of daily living. The majority, settling for the average, have resigned themselves to *just getting by*. Resignations to mediocrity have become a way of life. As a result, feelings of inadequacy cause many people, quite humanly, to blame others, society and circumstances for their failures and disappointments. The idea that other folks and things control their lives is so thoroughly ingrained in the thinking of these individuals that they will not respond to logical arguments, which prove otherwise.

Don Miguel Ruiz, M.D., author of *The Four Arguments*, teaches us from his Toltec wisdom that people often prefer to live in drama because it's comfortable. It's like someone staying in a bad marriage or relationship, it's actually easier to stay because they know what to expect everyday, versus leaving and not knowing what will happen next. Ruiz says that people have practiced being the way they are for years and years, and they know exactly how to do it. They feel safe even while they suffer. In contrast, when they go into the unknown, they feel fear. Sadly, happiness may be unknown. Love may be unknown. To open the heart in trust may also be an unknown experience. These people may say that *love hurts* without knowing it doesn't have to be that way.

Dr. Nathaniel Branden, the best-selling author of *The Psychology of Self-Esteem*, reminds us that there are realities in life that we cannot avoid. One of them is the importance of self-esteem. However, we can run from this profound truth if it makes us uncomfortable. We can wave it off, avoid it, proclaim that we are only interested in "practical" matters, and escape into sporting activities, the evening news, the financial pages, a shopping spree, or some other adventure.

Nevertheless, self-esteem is a fundamental need of all human beings. How we feel about ourselves crucially affects virtually every aspect of our experience, from the way we function at work or school to how we give and receive love, to how well we perform as parents, to how high in life we are likely to rise. Who we think we are will shape our responses to the happenings in our everyday life. Self-esteem is the key to success or failure.

Churnin' Milk into Butter

There were two frogs playing around in a pond—chasing one another, leaping from one lily pad to the next. The leading frog jumped from a lily pad onto the green pastures of a nearby farm. The trailing frog followed as he chased the first frog. The two frogs leaped, leaped, and leaped in a chase across the large pasture and then finally entered a barn full of hay bales and cows. The farmer milked his cows inside this particular barn.

The leading frog was enjoying the game, so he continued to leap. The second frog kept following. The two frogs, one after the other, leaped onto a stack of baled hay. Then they leaped up to a higher stack, then an even higher stack, until they reached the rafters near the inner roof of the barn. The first frog then hopped from one rafter over to the next as the second frog followed. The leader then came upon a jump where he miscalculated the distance to the next rafter. So he leaped, but came up short. The first frog plunged from the high rafter and landed in a five-gallon bucket of milk. He found himself surrounded by this unfamiliar white liquid substance. The frog didn't quite know how to respond to this unknown environment. He became scared and uncertain of himself. Thus he drowned.

The second frog, still chasing his friend, also misjudged the same distance to the next rafter. He plunged from the high place into a different five-gallon bucket of milk. Gadooosh! was the sound as he landed. This frog also found himself surrounded by the same white liquid substance. But, that didn't matter to him. He didn't care if the liquid was white, red, brown, or crystal-clear. He knew that he was a frog—a championship swimmer by nature! Tenaciously, this frog swam and kicked so long that he eventually churned the milk into butter. Then the trailing frog hopped right out of the bucket and commenced to search for his friend, the first frog.

In life, we are sometimes confronted with environments that are quite different than those we know well. Whether it's a new school, career, geographical location, business or relationship, just remember who you are. And even more importantly think of whose you are (belonging to those such as your family, deity, etc.). With these thoughts, you will come out on top of most adverse situations.

*"Don't complain about what you don't have. Use what you've got.
To do less than your best is a sin. Every single one of us has the
power for greatness, because greatness is determined by service—to
yourself and to others."*

—Oprah Winfrey

Monkey See, Monkey Do

We live in a Monkey See, Monkey Do world. We're told what the
latest fashions are, and we wear them. We hear the latest jargon,
and we make it the center post of our conversations. We mirror
our environments. We get most of our opinions from those
around us. Monkey See, Monkey Do.

Nowhere is this more apparent than with young people.
They go where their chosen in-crowd goes. They say what the in-
crowd says. They want to be accepted. In many ways this is
normal. You want to be liked, so you don't go against the group.
Of course, there's a group that goes against the group, but even
that's a clique of sorts.

We learn to conform, conform, and conform some more.
If this trend isn't broken, when our teenagers become adults,
nothing changes. They keep going along with the consensus of
the adult group, wanting the same things that the rest of the
group wants. Acceptance and peer approval supplants individuality. What gets lost in the shuffle is self-esteem. Belonging
becomes way more important than finding out who *we really are*
and what *we really think* about things.

In most cases, this lack of individuality has its roots in
childhood.

*"I'm not your average girl from a video; my worth is not determined
by the price of my clothes. But no matter what I'm wearing—I
will always be... India Arie."*

—India Arie

The Center of Attention

"Isn't he just the cutest thing!" "Look at that, little Naomi touched her nose. Isn't that amazing!" "Oh what a beautiful baby. You are so adorable!"

This is the way you were raised. You got attention for every gurgle, for every burp, for every little nuance. You were the apple of your daddy's eye, mama's pride and joy. You were the center of attention for the whole family. Love and adoration defined your world. In your little baby consciousness, you had to assume it would always be this way. You didn't have to do anything—just "be"—and the world showered you with love.

This is the way most of us came into the world. It's a set up. As we grew up, this default adoration became harder to come by. We began to question the love and attention that we had gotten earlier. For too many of us, self-esteem suffered and we developed masks that we could wear to hide our true feelings—in many cases even from ourselves. We started wearing these masks to school, adjusting them to blend in with the other masks.

These masks are holding us back. Self-esteem is hiding behind the mask—in too many cases, way behind the mask.

"Always be yourself. Those that matter won't mind. Those that mind won't matter."
—Anonymous

Born with Silver Spoons

As a kid, one of my favorite television shows in the 1980s was *Silver Spoons*. How lucky could a kid be? Ricky Schroeder lived in a mansion with his dad and servant, while being waited on hand and foot. He had all kinds of pinball machines and my favorite full-sized electronic games like Pac-Man, Donkey Kong, Centipede, and Asteroids. Ricky even had a choo-choo train on tracks that he often rode throughout the big house. Boy, I was jealous! His living room looked like a video arcade. His dad was wealthy and could afford whatever Ricky's heart desired. For most of my childhood, I was envious of Ricky—mainly because I was poor and underprivileged.

Some people are born with much more going for them. They come from wealthy, beautiful, talented, and intelligent folks. Interestingly, however, there's an amazing historical pattern that suggests some of the offspring of the rich and famous become huge failures. They are unable to achieve anything, to rise to the greatness of their heritage, to accept themselves, or to perform effectively in society on their own. This may be attributed to having so much going for them in the beginning that their inner-drive did not develop enough to carry them forward.

Yet some offspring in the most backward, discouraging environments have become productive high-achievers in every walk of life. One very important lesson is that *out of adversity can come greatness.*

Growing into Greatness:
Lady Eleanor's Path to Self-Esteem

"No matter how plain a woman may be—if truth & loyalty are stamped upon her face all will be attracted to her."
        —Eleanor Roosevelt, age 14

If anyone's story stands as a beacon for self-esteem, it's that of Eleanor Roosevelt. She was a shy, awkward child, starved for recognition and love, but she grew into one of the most competent women of the 20th Century, a woman with great sensitivity to the underprivileged who bravely worked through her timidity to champion the causes that she believed in. She had a dramatic, lasting impact on our country's policy toward youth, blacks, women, the poor, and the United Nations.

Anna Eleanor Roosevelt was born in New York City on October 11, 1884, the daughter of lovely Anna Hall and Elliott Roosevelt, younger brother of Theodore. The Roosevelts were a socially prominent family. Unfortunately, Eleanor had a very unhappy childhood. Her mother was a beauty, unlike her daughter, and she cruelly called the awkward Eleanor "granny." Her father, whom she adored, was an alcoholic, and was banished from the family. Her mother died when Eleanor was eight and two years later, her father died. Her grandmother Hall was very strict with Eleanor—which only added to Eleanor's insecurity. At fifteen, Eleanor was sent to Allenswood, a distinguished finishing school in England, which gave Eleanor her first chance to develop a sense of self-esteem. The headmistress, Marie Souvestre, encouraged Eleanor to come out of her shell and become a school leader—and she did.

Eleanor returned to New York in 1902 to make the society debut that she dreaded. Already her social consciousness was evident, as she preferred working with the poor of the city in a settlement house to the trappings of the elite. A distant cousin, Franklin Delano Roosevelt, was in her circle of friends. They were engaged in 1903 and married two years later. Teddy Roosevelt gave the bride away. Within eleven years, Eleanor bore six children, losing one in infancy. She would later write in her autobiography: "I suppose I was fitting pretty well into the pattern of a fairly conventional, quiet, young society matron."

Franklin served in the New York state Senate from 1910-1913, and Eleanor played the role of helpmate, a role that she would know all too well for the next thirty years. Later, when FDR served as Assistant Secretary of the Navy during WWI, she did volunteer work with the Red Cross and began to understand how things worked in the nation's capitol. She played well her part as the wife of a politician.

This changed at the end of the war. She discovered that her husband had a serious affair with another woman. Eleanor and Franklin reconciled, but Eleanor became determined to have a life of her own. Through the years, even though she remained dedicated to FDR's purposes, she definitely made her opinions known and carved out her own course.

Franklin was stricken with poliomyelitis in 1921. Eleanor took care of him with great devotion and made sure that his interest in politics stayed alive. Eleanor had become very active in personal causes. She was part of the League of Woman Voters, the Women's Trade Union League, and the women's division of the Democratic Party. Eleanor became her husband's political stand-in. In 1928, FDR reentered the political arena, running successfully for governor of New York. By that time his wife was herself a political figure to be reckoned with.

When her husband became president in 1933, at first she

was afraid that being first lady would be confining, but thankfully, she was determined to do it her way. She transformed the role of first lady. This former wallflower didn't shy away from entertaining, she held her own press conferences, gave lectures, had a radio program and a daily syndicated newspaper column entitled *My Day*.

She also traveled the country over, becoming the eyes and ears for her husband. She became a tireless spokeswoman for the cause of the underprivileged. This outspoken, precedent-setting woman was an easy target for enemies of the administration, but her integrity and her sincerity endeared her to millions—from heads of states to the troops she visited in WWII to the common people she touched along the way.

In 1945 FDR died. Eleanor returned to a cottage in Hyde Park and declared, "The story is over." Within a year, however, she began her service as American spokeswoman in the United Nations. This began seventeen more years of public service, some of which were the most satisfactory of her career. She was appointed by President Harry Truman a member of the U.S. delegation to the United Nations in December 1945, and then later reappointed by JFK. In between, she served as Chairperson of the Commission of Human Rights. She remained active in Democratic Party politics.

In her later years, Eleanor Roosevelt presided over her large family at her home in Hyde Park. She continued a vigorous career, kept up a voluminous correspondence and an active social life. *"I suppose I should slow down,"* she said on her seventy-seventh birthday, and soon she did. Her strength began to wane the following year. She died in New York City on November 7, 1962 and was buried in the rose garden at Hyde Park beside her husband.

Her many books include, *This Is My Story* (1937), *This I Remember* (1949), and *On My Own* (1958). Each of these great works chronicled her development of self-esteem. As it was with Eleanor Roosevelt, many of us are not raised in an atmosphere of self-esteem. We must wade through the injustice of our upbringing and fight our way to the mirror of self-love and appreciation.

Lady Eleanor was one of America's great reforming leaders and an important public personality in her own right.

This formerly awkward wallflower taught me one of the most important lessons in my life: she said, *"Learn from the mistakes of others. You can't live long enough to make them all yourself."*

"No one can make you feel inferior without your consent."
    —Lady Eleanor Roosevelt

The Importance of Self-Esteem

Nathaniel Branden was the first to coin the phrase "self-esteem" back in the 1950's. Although it can be said fifty years later that this term has been bandied around too casually—often being a sugar coating for narcissism—the importance of self-esteem in our daily and professional lives can't be denied. Respect and appreciation for one's self is at the heart of human affairs. If I don't like who I am, I will not like who you are either. I may fake it, I may even compensate in some co-dependent manner, but it won't hold.

I feel true self-esteem is important in all aspects of our lives. It's the soft center in the tootsie pop, the heart of the artichoke. Self-esteem is like petroleum in your favorite car; if you're low on gas—you won't be traveling very far. Without high self-esteem our lives become a perpetual search for approval and aggrandizement.

If your self-esteem is low, how do you develop it? As I already mentioned, you learn who you are very early in life. You're not born with feelings of inferiority—you adopt them. The most important key to self-esteem is the untying of your seeming status in the world from your feelings of self worth. Outward success, physical appearance, social status, overt beauty or any other outside condition does not determine self-esteem. Self-esteem is a direct outreach from your values. How honest are you in your life? How strong is your integrity? How responsible are your actions?

Taking responsibility for your choices, your feelings and your actions promotes a feeling a self worth. In short, you control the gateway to self-esteem.

How conscious are you about the way you live your life? Do you go through your days with your eyes open? Or do you keep your blinders on? Positive self-esteem is a direct reflection of the appropriateness of your thoughts and actions. Do you meet challenges head on? Or do you shirk them? Do you live from your convictions? Or do your values work on a sliding scale?

In my estimation, the more "real" a person is—the bigger their dose of reality—the higher their self-esteem.

If you want to raise your self-esteem, raise the esteem in others. Praise the people in your life. First of all, they deserve it. Secondly, it will automatically raise the esteem you have for yourself. Our friends and family, associates and community are mirrors. Find something of value in everyone you encounter and you value yourself accordingly. Every human being deserves your respect. Every human being has value. If you have trouble seeing it in you, start by seeing it in us and the ball will begin to roll in the right direction.

Is self-acceptance the same as self-esteem? In the same way that confidence depends on trust, self-esteem is an outgrowth of acceptance. If you don't first truly accept who you are—the beauty and the warts—appreciation and esteem don't have a breeding ground. As Nathaniel Branden says, *"Self-acceptance is a refusal to deny or disown any aspect of the self: our thoughts, emotions, memories, physical attributes, sub-personalities, or actions."*

You need to be able to stand naked in front of the mirror and say, "Hello me. I see you, I really see you and I fully accept you." Any judgment that you have about yourself is a shadow on your self-esteem.

Needless to say, the process of self-acceptance isn't easy. It takes understanding. And it takes great courage. You need to be the No. 1 cheerleader in your life.

Self-esteem = self-love=self-confidence=self-respect. When you live your life according to your values and your rules—in other words, when you live authentically—you feel good about who you are. You know who you are. You find it easier to take your place in the world. It's easier to follow your destiny, to express yourself, to create the life of your dreams. Self-esteem leads to self-expression.

Do you have to like all your personalities? Every one of us has a whole roster of sub-personalities. For most of us, some of these personas are disowned, unrecognized or denied. If you want to juice your esteem, you have to invite all these personalities to come out of the closet and play. Let them join the party. Each of them has something important to contribute. However, when you do it, you need to acknowledge them, befriend them, and ultimately embrace them.

This ritual of acceptance leads to wholeness and wholeness breeds self-esteem.

Do unto others. In both your personal and your professional life, the Golden Rule is the code—especially if you want to stoke your feelings of self worth. Treat others the way you want to be treated and it's guaranteed you'll feel better about you and you'll get the kind of feedback that reinforces that feeling.

This is particularly true in business. Treat your fellow workers and employees exactly as you treat your customers. (Granted, there are way too many companies out there that treat their customers like gross inconveniences, but you get the idea.) In business, you can have temporary success without having a podium of self-esteem, but it will be short-lived. The workers who rise to the top feel good about themselves and know that whatever success they have in business does not define them. How they feel about themselves defines them.

Self-esteem is a habit. And like all habits, there is a learning curve. Letting go of the old opinion of self and replacing it with the new, improved model takes time and requires courage. You're asking yourself to go to the edge of the comfort zone where it's not as cushy, and step into the great unknown. Two steps forward, one back. Part of the time you'll be fighting the demons of the past who seem to be dedicated to pulling you back to your old ways, but persevere, it's only a matter of time before you start to feel comfortable in your new skin.

The people in your life. Understand something, as you grow and evolve—which is a definite bi-product of raising your self-esteem—your family, friends and associates may not know how to react. They've been used to a different version of you, more-than-likely one they're comfortable with, one that is predictable to them. Suddenly, you're more cheerful, more self-assured, more open and less defensive. You'd think your friends would be happy about this, but it doesn't always work that way. We attract people to our lives for a myriad of reasons. One of them has to do with matching attitudes and beliefs. When you upgrade your inner value, you present a new mirror to the people in your world, and not everybody is going to like the reflection.

Some will adjust—some may not. No matter what, the world as you've known it will never be the same. Welcome to your destiny. Welcome to the fast lane.

"The higher your self-esteem, the more inclined you are to treat others with respect, benevolence, and goodwill."
—Nathaniel Branden

Your Five-Step Self-Esteem Course of Action

Plan to:

1. Reserve time to conquer your fears: Recall the V.I.P.E.R. method: *Verbalize, Imagine, Practice, Experience* and *Relax* while overcoming your fears.

2. Generate a positive belief system for yourself at school, at work, and at home: Evaluate your attitude. It affects everything you do and how you relate to others.

3. Concentrate on your marketable strengths: Ask yourself these three powerful questions: *Who am I? Am I really who I am?* And, *Am I all I ought to be?* Concentrate on your strengths, special hobbies, education, work, and relationships. Examine your facial expressions, tone of voice, posture, stance, and gestures. They convey exactly who we are to others.

4. Create time to dream and plan: Make this a habit. Set daily, weekly, and monthly goals. Develop a road map of activities and

plan for how you'll get from where you are to where you want to go.

5. Do it right now by taking action: Practice the T-N-T method - *"today, not tomorrow."* Strengthen your mind, seek new challenges and responsibilities, and take advantage of what you know.

"Nobody can dim the light which shines from within."
—Dr. Maya Angelou

Now, to help you raise your level of self-esteem, complete the following exercise and then read on.

LIFE-ESSENTIAL THREE EXERCISE

1. Do you perceive yourself as successful? Are your thoughts consistent with your actions? What aspects of your life need special attention?

2. List five negative messages that you remember hearing as a child or messages that you hear today.

3. Now take these same five negative statements and turn them into positive ones. Place all five statements on 3 x 5 cards and repeat the positive statements twice daily.

4. Write three positive words that describe you.

5. What was the most positive message your parents gave you?

6. What would you most like to be remembered for in your life?

7. List briefly what you are most proud of:

A difficult job...

A goal you reached...

An award you received...

A compliment you gave...

A habit you changed...

LIFE-ESSENTIAL 4

MOVING FROM IMPOSSIBLE TO I'MPOSSIBLE

Navigating through Life's Changes

"Ordinary people believe only in the possible. Extraordinary people visualize not what is possible or probable, but rather what is impossible. And by visualizing the impossible, they begin to see it as possible."

—Cherie Carter-Scott

There's one thing that all of us want, all of the time, for any number of reasons: CHANGE! And there's one thing that is nearly impossible for the average person to handle gracefully: CHANGE! Change is the great conundrum. We want to be better human beings, better parents, better mates, better providers. We want to lose weight, make friends, eat better, feel better, be better.

We want to change, but it's not easy for most of us.

Although we want to change, many of us hang on to weighty things in our lives. We scratch an issue like it's an irritating itch. At the moment, we may not be in complete suffering, but then again, we're not really getting the relief we wish for either.

The itch can come and go away periodically, but the more we think about it, the more it irritates us. We settle for our lives, as they are. We put up with the itching; hoping things will magically get better. But an itch doesn't get better just by scratching it, and the irritations in our lives only get worse until something is done to improve the situation.

Not that you can't live with the itch. You can. You can make do in your life, and rationalize the itch away. You can get so used to the itch, that it hardly bothers you anymore. "Hardly" is the key word here. This is the way most of us get by. "Hardly" living.

This is a very important chapter in the book. I want you to master change. I want you to give up "hardly." Strike it from your vocabulary. Now if you're saying back to me—"Tony, what's a little itch? My life isn't so bad... it's not perfect, but I can get by" —then close the book, throw it away. But if it's time to move on...read on.

I want you to be a change-maker. I want you to quit scratching and get to the source. I want you to get so good at change that when it's time to make one, you don't even have to think about it. I want you to master change so that you can master your life.

"Smooth seas do not make skillful sailors."
—An African Proverb

Carrots, Eggs, & Coffee Beans

A young woman complained to her father about how things were so hard for her. This woman didn't know how she was going to make it and wanted to give up. She was tired of fighting and struggling. It seemed as if one problem was solved only to have a new one rise up.

Her father, a chef, took her to the kitchen. He filled three pots with water and placed each on a high fire. Soon the pots came to a boil. In one he placed carrots, in the second he placed eggs, and in the last he placed ground coffee beans. He let them sit and boil without saying a word.

The daughter sucked her teeth and impatiently waited, wondering what he was doing. In about twenty minutes, he turned off the burners. Her father fished the carrots out and placed them in a bowl. He pulled the eggs out and placed them in a bowl. Then he ladled the coffee out and placed it in a mug.

Turning to her, he asked, "Darling, what do you see?"

"Carrots, eggs, and coffee," she replied.

He brought his daughter closer and asked her to feel the carrots. She did and noted that they were soft. He then asked her to take an egg and break it. After pulling off the shell, she observed the hard-boiled egg. Finally, he asked her to sip the coffee. The daughter smiled, as she tasted its rich flavor.

She humbly asked, "What does it mean, Father?"

He explained that each of them had faced the same adversity, boiling water, but each reacted differently.

The carrots went in strong, hard, and unrelenting. But after being subjected to the boiling water, they softened and became weak.

The eggs had been fragile. Their thin outer shells had protected the liquid interiors. But after sitting through the boiling water, the insides had become hardened.

The ground coffee beans were unique. After being boiled, they changed the water.

"Which are you?" he asked his daughter. "When adversity knocks on your door, how do you respond? Are you a carrot, an egg, or a coffee bean?"

How about you, my friend? Are you the carrot that seems hard, but becomes weak and soft with adversity?

Are you the egg, which started off with a malleable heart? Did you have a fluid inner spirit, but after the loss of a loved one, a breakup, a divorce, or a layoff, has your spirit stiffened? Does your outer shell look the same as before, but inside you are bitter and tough with a hardened heart?

Or are you like the coffee bean? The bean changes the hot water—the thing that is bringing the pain—and reaches its peak flavor at 212 degrees Fahrenheit. When the water gets the hottest—the coffee tastes its best.

So if you are like the coffee bean, when things are at their worst, you will get better and make things around you better too.

How do you handle adversity? Are you a carrot, an egg, or a coffee bean?

"Your results have been determined by your beliefs. Change your beliefs and you will change your results."
　—Larry Winget

Welcome to the Twenty-First Century: The Here & Now

The abacus—an instrument for performing calculations by sliding counters along rods or in grooves—was invented in what is now Iraq in the fourth century B. C. In some parts of the world, the abacus is still used today.

The first general purpose programmable calculator was invented by a German engineer, Konrad Zuse, in 1941. This calculator pioneered the use of binary math and Boolean logic in electronic calculation.

The IBM 360 was introduced in April of 1964. It quickly became the standard institutional mainframe computer. (In the next twenty years, the 360 and its descendants generated more than $100 billion in revenue for IBM.) The first computers took up half a room and had just a fraction of the convenient speed and capability of the laptop that you carry to Starbucks.

When I went to college, in my engineering courses, I was able to use a calculator for my computations, but a generation earlier, my colleagues were using a slide rule to work out the same problems. (My good friend Jack, who graduated in Mechanical Engineering in the mid-60s, says that the only thing he's retained from his education was how to use a slide rule and it's been out-of-date for thirty years!)

Why am I telling you all this?

We're now in the Twenty-First Century. It would be downright ignorant to use an abacus, a slide rule or even an IBM 360 to handle business, and keep our personal lives on course, if we had available to us a sleek, light-weight, modern, 40 gig personal computer. Yet, within our personal lives, this is the way we too often process everyday events. We grunt and groan and grit our teeth and grimace and grouse about the things that show up on our personal *movie screen*. In the normal course of events, in just living our lives, there will be rejections, dejections, disappointments, and dashed dreams. If we want destined lives, we have to deal with setbacks and move on.

Here's what I say: welcome to the Twenty-First Century! Excuse my metaphor—but throw the abacus away, and the slide rule, and all of the old, outdated modes of processing your life and come into the present moment. In the here and now...

Here...now... here...now... here...now. That's the speed of today's computers, and it should be the speed at which you navigate changes.

I have observed that the people who are best at using PC-processing in their lives—instead of abacus-processing—are happier, more prosperous, and even seem to be luckier than the rest. Do you think that's by coincidence? (On the subject of luck, as far as I'm concerned, luck is a term that losers use to describe winners.) People, who process the events of their lives quickly and don't hang on to what-might-have-been, accomplish more in a shorter period of time than others. They don't let the vicissitudes of living throw them off course. They master change.

The fairy tales were wrong, and they did us a great disservice. There is no Santa, no Easter bunny, no dashing charming prince, no beautiful princess waiting to be rescued. There is no happily ever-after. We would have been better served if we were taught that "life will be whatever you make it...and...along the way there will be seventy-eight rejections, forty-six colds, you'll get the flu a dozen times and have ten flat tires." So when a flat tire comes along, you can say: "Hooray, I got a flat tire, nine more to go!" Take the shortcut.

Change isn't always easy, no question about that, but when life deals a back hand—and you're going to get your share of back hands—use that fantastic inner computer and process it. Deal with your changes in the here and now... here...now... here ...now here...now...!

"Most of my major disappointments have turned out to be blessings in disguise. So whenever anything bad does happen to me, I kind of sit back and feel, well, if I give this enough time, it'll turn out that this was good, so I shouldn't worry about it too much."

—William Gaines

Mastering Change

"Open your arms to change, but don't let go of your values."

—Dalai Lama

Change is the one thing in life that is not going to change. No matter what you think, no matter how you want it to be, *things are going to change.* You can count on it. So if you want to stay on top of your world, you have to be a Master of Change.

In order to master something as seemingly unpredictable as change, you need to know the Conditions of Change, and before you can even begin to grasp their intricacies, you have to do the prep work. If you haven't done the prep work, when you're in the fray of the battle and have to go with the flow of change, you'll wilt like a daisy in the desert.

Prep Work for Change Mastery...

- Take your blinders off... see things for the way they really are.

- Shatter excuses in your life... drop your convenient stories, and all the oh-so-dramatic reasons you can't get it together.

- Upgrade your habits... if your habits aren't going to lead you to your dreams, either downgrade your dreams or upgrade your habits.

- Be grateful... for you, for us, for everything...especially for the vicissitudes of life. You've got to love change to master it.

The payoff for mastering change is freedom. If you can flow with change, you're way ahead of the game. Most of us are hanging on for dear life, gripping the status quo so tightly that are knuckles are whiter than granny's hair. Change-mastery is directly linked to self-love and self-reliance. The more able we are to depend on ourselves, the more prepared we are for change. As we talked about in the last chapter, self-esteem and self-respect are the most important prerequisites for the evolution of your life.

Read the following Conditions of Change and know that you can master change in the same way that you've mastered other things in your life.

"You are what your are and where you are because of what has gone into your mind, and you can change what you are and where you are by changing what goes into your mind."

—Zig Ziglar

The Conditions of Change

Count your victories. When confronted with a big change in your life, take a moment to tote up your latest wins— big and small. This prepares you for the windstorm that often accompanies change.

Do what you love; love what you do. I know you've already heard this but it's a truism. If you're not doing what you really love to do, making a change—unless it's in the direction of your destiny—can feel like water torture.

Feelings first. Any change—especially major change— requires that we face the feelings and emotions that show up. If you're not willing to touch in with your feelings, and express them when appropriate, you're not going to master change. Period.

Give credit where credit is due. No matter what happens, if you have the courage to go through change, give yourself a blue ribbon for trying. Only the brave are willing to go up to the dragon of change and ask him for a kiss.

Love yourself, love yourself, love yourself. And while you're at it include *us* in your love nest. Self love and respect is the ticket, whatever the show may be.

Risk, risk, risk. When a positive, albeit challenging change requires risk, don't hesitate. Leap! There is no safety net, and thank God you don't need one! As one of my favorite philosophers, the Dalai Lama says, "great love and great achievements involve great risk."

Take the high road. When confronted with the choices that change brings, make the choice that conforms most with your values and ideals.

Trust your instincts. You—and you alone—know what's best for your life. Tune in, determine what feels right and change will be exhilarating, not exhausting.

What's the worst thing that can happen? Write it down, create a solution-oriented contingency plan. If you're prepared for the worst thing that can happen, the reality is easier.

Being able to make changes gracefully requires that we know how to make choices, and unfortunately you don't get that in your education. Look around. The people you admire— the entrepreneurs, pathfinders, pioneers, celebrities—they are masters of change. They know who's writing their life script, and they also know that half of the script is improvised. There is nothing more boring—and demeaning—than the status quo.

Mastering change has great payoffs: self knowledge, self respect, self confidence, self esteem...not-to-mention that mastering change is the shortcut to fulfilling your destiny.

The bottom line is freedom. You came to this planet with the blueprint of freedom and fulfillment. If you've been change-phobic up to now, like anything worthwhile, mastering change is going to take practice. Experiment, take baby steps, be gentle with yourself, but know this: you are a master of change and it's about time that you knew it!

"Beliefs generate your thoughts and emotions, which create your experiences. To change your life, change your beliefs."
—Dick Sutphen

Bustin' Up Out of Your Cage

In the fall of 1993, I had the distinct privilege of personally escorting Dr. Maya Angelou for the evening as she graced Cal State Northridge with her stellar poetic performance for the Los Angeles community at large. As Jimmy Walker from the TV sitcom, *Good Times* would say, "It was dyn-o-mite!"

Maya spoke about her many literary works and reiterated the many reasons *why the caged bird sang*—she being that caged bird. I remember holding her hand with excitement as I helped Dr. Angelou around the Matadome Arena. On her hand, she wore this beautiful solid gold ring with a life-sized canary-like bird mounted on the top—I recall it specifically, because I nicked my finger on it from holding her hand so tight. This was a night that I will never forget—mainly because of her strong presence and life-inspiring words. Maya spoke of her young life filled with disappointment, frustration, tragedy, and how through strength of mind and lots of prayer—she prevailed.

Maya Angelou was born April 4, 1928 in Saint Louis, Missouri but was mostly raised in segregated rural Arkansas. Her name at birth was Marguerite Johnson. It was not until the age of twenty-five, dancing at the Purple Onion nightclub in San Francisco, that she adopted the name Maya Angelou. (Maya is what her brother called her in childhood, and Angelou was a corruption of her married name.)

Especially when it comes to facing extreme change and mastering it, Maya Angelou is a shining example for all of us. She has dealt with serious misfortune, eventually using it as the breeding ground for her prodigious talents.

Maya's parents divorced when she was three. She was sent with her brother, Bailey, to Stamps, Arkansas to live with their grandmother. Just like with my grandmother, they called theirs "Mama," and this Mama also had a deep-unconditional love that was real and rehabilitating for her grandkids.

As much love as there was in Maya's home environment, especially at that time in Arkansas, the white population was in control. Maya was a black girl living by the rules of a different culture. She wore old beat-up clothes handed down to her from white women. A white dentist refused her treatment. The whites looked down upon her. You can imagine the effect this sort of treatment had on an impressionable young girl. Like so many little black girls at that time, Maya dreamed of having long, smooth, unkinky blond hair. Thankfully, her grandma helped Maya find esteem and confidence through the love of God—the pillar of strength in their little family.

Maya and Bailey stayed with their grandma for five years before they were reunited with their mother in Chicago. During this time, Maya experienced a truly dark moment in her life. She was severely raped by her mother's boyfriend—who was subsequently murdered. Maya refused to speak to anyone but her brother for the next four years. She and her brother were sent back to Stamps, Arkansas to be with her grandma—"Mama"— the only one who could help Maya heal her emotional wounds.

Mama's love and the mentoring of a nice lady named Mrs. Flowers had an uplifting effect on Maya. Slowly she developed into an alive and vibrant young girl—filled with pride and self-esteem.

Then in 1940, as before, she was sent to live with her unfit mother, this time in San Francisco. Her mother's life was too chaotic for Maya to handle, so she moved in with her father and his lady friend in his broken-down trailer home. Life with her father was no better than it was with her mother, and Maya ended up with dozens of other homeless kids in an abandoned lot full of wrecked vehicles. The self-esteem that Maya had begun to experience in Arkansas with her grandma was diminished by the chaos of her life in the Bay Area. Trying to survive her confusing situation, she hurried her maturity, dropped out of high school and became the first black cable car conductor in San Francisco. She also became pregnant at the age of sixteen and had a son she named Guy.

This period of Maya's life was tumultuous. As a young mother, between the age of sixteen and twenty-five, Maya was a Creole cook, a madam, a tap dancer, a chauffeur and had a brief flirtation with drugs and prostitution. At the age of twenty-four, she married Tosh Angelos, a white ex-sailor—and a dependable source of stability for Maya and young Guy. Their marriage would end in divorce five years later—Maya would choose her career as a dancer over her marriage with Tosh.

This was a pivotal time in Maya's life. Her career—which would eventually birth so many incarnations—was just beginning to take off, and Maya was filled with guilt over her neglect of Guy. It nearly drove her to suicide, but she survived. Maya Angelou is a survivor, and to our betterment has shared her turbulent and inspiring journey with all of us.

Today, Maya Angelou is an internationally respected poet, writer and educator, who has given us such best-selling titles as *I Know Why the Caged Bird Sings, Gather Together in My Name, Singin' and Swingin' and Gettin' Merry Like Christmas* and *The Heart of a Woman*. She produced and starred in the great play *Cabaret for Freedom* and starred in *The Blacks*. She wrote the original screenplay and musical score for the film *Georgia, Georgia* and was both author and executive producer of a five-part television mini-series, *Three Way Choice*. This list barely touches her accomplishments. She is a magnificent, multi-talented woman.

Dancer, singer, poet, actress, screenwriter, author, lecturer, director, producer—Maya Angelou has navigated through life's changes and paved the way for the rest of us to do the same. If Maya can deal with the hand that was dealt her, and make it a winner, why can't we?

Over the years, Dr. Maya Angelou has become quite a phenomenon. Among her accomplishments are the mentoring of great individuals like Oprah Winfrey; teaching the written and spoken word to thousands of college students; authoring many books, poems, plays, and essays; and inspiring the United States of America and the world community at large with her inaugural poem *On the Pulse of Morning*, commissioned by President William Jefferson Clinton. She greatly inspires me and is indeed my "shero".

As Maya Angelou spoke that evening about coming out of her cage, I was certain that millions of other people were struggling within their cages too. I know I have. I've learned that it takes a C.A.G.E. to bust up out of your cage. If you want to have a life of freedom and fulfillment—turn to C.A.G.E. as another self-defining acronym that will give you the combination to unlock the door of the cage that's keeping you from maximizing your potential.

C is for **Change**. Change your mind and your behind will follow.

A is for **Act**. Once you set your mind to do something, then DO IT!

G is for **Grow**. Plant your roots right where you are and grow from there.

E is for **Evolve**. Learn from every human experience, make every experience work for you in some way, shape, form, or fashion.

Just like Maya Angelou, you too can break out of your cage by using this formula.

"You wanna know why you keep on attracting the same old tired mess to your life? It's because you are the same old tired person."
—Dr. Maya Angelou

Life's Like an Etch-O-Sketch

Watching the movie *Toy Story* with my children brought back memories of the *Etch-O-Sketch* game my Aunt Glenda bought me for Christmas one year. Can you recall that thin red box with those white knobs that were used to draw designs on the larger gray board? Remember how you'd have to turn it upside down, shake it all around from side to side, and then sometimes bang the sides to erase the canvas? It was always amazing to me when someone would write their name in cursive, draw a house with flowers and trees, or sketch an animal or whatever. It didn't matter to me how skilled or unskilled you were with the Etch-O-Sketch, as long as you made anything look like something —then you were good in my book. I just thought it was the neatest toy.

As an adult, I see the Etch-O-Sketch as a metaphor for everyday life. As everyday people, we have our daily ups and downs—confusion and drama. We generally start out the day with intentions to make it a happy one, but sometimes it doesn't go exactly the way we designed it in our minds. Something goes wrong. Someone cuts you off in traffic. You forget your wallet or purse. You lock yourself out of the house or car. You don't pass that important test. You don't receive your promotion. Your team doesn't win the big game. Someone forgets your birthday or anniversary.

Well, just like with an Etch-O-Sketch, while "drawing" our lives we face obstacles, make mistakes, and sometimes we end up with rather ugly pictures. That's the beautiful thing about an Etch-O-Sketch. When you're not quite happy with the way your design turned out, you can just shake that thing up, erase the board and start over. You never have to stick to the previous design. It can always be changed.

You have to learn to get over certain things. Just throw them over your shoulder and start again. I believe you are worth it!

"No matter how spotted our past, our future is spotless."
—Anonymous

René the Village "Super" Hero

Born in a tiny, isolated village on the island of Haiti, my good friend René Godefroy was an impoverished child perpetually tormented by cholera, rickets, and malnutrition. Abandoned by his father and left behind while his mother sought work in the city, René subsisted on meager charity, bread, fruit, and the rare fish he caught with a string and hook. Some people of his village called him "Souyan," which means a sick and disabled old man. Few expected that he would survive to adulthood.

René surprised them. In 1983, at the age of twenty-one, he came to Montreal with a Haitian theater company and escaped into the United States wedged between the tires of a tractor-trailer. He arrived in New York City with five dollars in his pocket and two shirts and a pair of pants in his battered suit-case. In the years that followed, René supported himself by doing hard labor for low pay. All the while, in his heart, Rene knew that he was capable of much more. René taught himself English, read voraciously, and dedicated himself to his grandest ambition. Today, he is a proud citizen of the United States, a successful businessman, a motivational speaker and an inspiring author. When the man they called "Souyan" returned to visit Haiti, a man told him, "You are our Village Hero."

René's whole life experience is his message to the world—that "No Condition is Permanent!"—the title of his best-selling book. René personifies the old adage —*no test, no testimony.*

"You can be a dreamer and a doer too if you remove one word from your vocabulary: Impossible!"
—Dr. Robert H. Schuller

Just Let Your Feet Decide

Before you get all stirred up inside
Before you summon your pride
Before you go off all cockeyed
Take it in stride...let your feet decide

At approximately 8:45 pm on October 2nd, 2002, I received a frantic phone call from my younger cousin Dana. I could tell immediately that something was wrong—she couldn't quite get it out. She asked, *"Tony—did you hear about our cousin Man?"* This cousin's real name was James Harris Taplin, Jr., but we affectionately called him *"Man"*. I replied with great concern, *"No! What happened?"* Dana answered with heartbreak in her voice, *"Man died."* *"How did he die?"*—I asked in disbelief. She told me Man had been killed in a drive-by shooting!

Earlier that evening, Man had just made it in from working all day doing construction work with Uncle Earl. He was at home relaxing with our grandmother, Mama, who he lived with and looked after. Close to 8:00 pm that night, Man told Mama: *"I'll be right back. I'm gonna go 'round the corner for a minute."* Mama replied with no worries, *"All right now, I'll see you when you get back."* While coming back home from visiting his friends from around the corner, Man innocently stepped into the wrong place at the wrong time. He actually walked right into a drive-by targeted for another individual!

The LAPD and the local community suspect that local *Crip* gang members drove through the Nickerson Gardens Housing Projects—home to a rival *Blood* gang known notoriously as the Bounty Hunters—and shot up the block. At 6 feet 5 inches tall, and weighing roughly 300 pounds, Man had made a huge target. They shot my cousin four times with a 9 mm semi-automatic weapon in the back and once in his upper leg with an AK-47 assault rifle. Man died at the scene—just three weeks before his thirty-second birthday.

In addition to the nickname "Man," friends and neighbors had also lovingly called my cousin *"Baby Huey,"* because he was a huge and lovable guy with an enormous heart—*just like the big baby duck cartoon character that only wanted to be your friend.* Man was also the father of a nine-year-old son. Sadly, an endless scourge of killings of and by African-Americans is little noticed elsewhere, but those who must live with the aftermath are changed forever.

Events like these tend to bring out society's shadow-side. As if losing Man wasn't difficult enough, my family had to put up with lies, rumors and gossip that so often accompanies these kinds of tragedies. As we were dealing with Man's death, we were also confronted by the shortsightedness in people.

I'm proud of my family. In the midst of the pain and suffering, through the funeral and grieving, we endured the indignities with grace and self-respect.

> *Before you go off somewhere to hide*
> *Before you start the downward slide*
> *Remember who you are, face your future*
> *And let your feet decide*

I call this principle: *Let Your Feet Decide.* You can't let other people's thoughts, words, and opinions stop you. Because, if they do—they always will. People will think whatever they feel like thinking. And you can't stop the talking. People think they need something juicy to talk about. This is their problem, not yours, unless you make it so. Don't let the rest of the world decide your fate, let your feet decide. Your feet know the way to your future. Don't get thrown off course. In your lifetime, you will have more than your share of adversity, and the people in and around your life will say what they say and you can't change it.

What you can change is how you respond to it, and where you invest your attention.

> *Before you scream: "Not right, he lied,"*
> *"Lord knows, I tried"*
> *Give the problem to your feet*
> *And let your feet decide*

Walk away and keep on walking. If you know the direction of your destiny, tell your feet to keep moving that way. As my Grandmother used to say, "Whatever you survive—only makes you stronger" and when it comes to what other people think, take the advice from First Lady Eleanor Roosevelt. She said, *"Don't worry so much about what other people think—because they seldom do."* The best way to survive this kind of torment is to be bigger than their littleness, and to keep on walking in the direction of your dreams. Give the problem to your feet, and let your feet decide.

No matter how hard, no matter how unfair, don't get thrown off course. Life travels on a sine wave. Up and down, up and down, and up and down some more. That's not going to change. You really need to know who you are and what you stand for when it's your turn for another "down". Focus on your bright future and stay the course.

> *When right and reason collide*
> *When a "response" seems so justified*
> *Turn around, take a breath*
> *Let your feet be your guide*

All of my life, people have asked me how I managed to escape the clutches of wretchedness, poverty, and violence. How did I survive the abandonment by my mother's death at a young age and still finish high school? How did I get through engineering school and business school? How did I make it past toxic relationships with relatives and so-called friends? How did I find such a beautiful bride and family of my own? Guess what I told them all—I just kept on walking in the direction of my dreams.

This doesn't mean that you don't cry or hurt during the process. It doesn't mean it'll be that easy—but you've just got to keep on going—keep on walking. If you give up now, you'll never get what you're after. There is something worthy in your future that is stronger than your past. No matter how ugly, muddy, filthy, murky, gloomy, or spotted your past has been—always remember your future is spotless. There is a nation of greatness within you. Do yourself this favor. Don't die before you witness your own greatness. As long as you have feet—let them decide, then keep on walking! Just keep on walking...

> *Before you get all snivelly and snide*
> *Before you say something truly undignified*
> *Ask your feet how important this is*
> *And let your feet decide*

No Way... My Way... Gateway... Freeway...

In a way, experiencing change is exactly the same as experiencing loss. When you've lost something of value in your life—for example, your home burns down or you lose a loved one—you go through a forced change. Even when the stakes aren't quite that high, the process of any kind of change has four distinct phases:

No Way: This isn't really happening.

My Way: I'm under attack, I need to hold onto what's near and dear.

Gateway: OK, let me see what this is all about.

Freeway: Wheeee... this isn't so bad, let's go for it.

I call the first phase **No Way**. You're in a state of shock. This isn't really happening. If you just close your eyes tight enough and turn away from the fire, bury yourself in comfort food, turn the TV up to its full volume, get nice and cuddly under the covers, it will all go away. It's just a bad dream.

In a lot of ways, this is normal. (Keep in mind, I'm not a big fan of "normal." It's "normal" to do a lot of things, but "normal" doesn't usually move the ball ahead.) The *No Way* demon has many faces. First you deny it's happening (not me), then you try to brush it aside (ignorance is bliss), then when it's ugly head pops up again, which it will, you minimize it (if I do just a little fine tuning, it will be peachy keen).

Regardless of how good you are at the *No Way* phase, eventually it becomes clear that change is underway. What's your response?

You go into the **My Way** phase. In this phase, it all gets worse. You begin to resist. You lash out. Surely there's someone to blame for this indignity that you're enduring. You see this a lot in business when a major shift occurs. Most everybody finds someone to blame for it. (Of course, in business there is always a convenient scapegoat up the line to take the rap.)

It's not unusual in the *My Way* phase to break down, to become physically ill or emotionally upset. This is a tough transition. I call it *My Way* because we're trying so hard to hold onto to what we think is real, to not have to change. "At all costs, I need to continue to do it my way." (My apologies to Frank Sinatra. *My Way* may be a nice song, but it's not a nice way to confront life.)

Buried at the bottom of the pile is a voice whispering "it's over, life as you know it will never be again" but you're more focused on crying about the past than you are on adjusting to this change. You may even slip back into the *No Way* phase.

Thankfully, nothing lasts forever. One of two things is going to happen: 1) you're either going to create great distress or disease in you life, or 2) you're going to move on.

The next phase I call the **Gateway**. Once you face up to what's happening in your life and admit how you feel, you start to feel better about things. You come to the gateway and walk through. You let go of the despair and judgment and begin to explore your possibilities. You realize that you're going to survive. You go to the drawing board and open up to the potential of your new situation.

You accept the change.

The last phase I call the **Freeway**. Once you've accepted that change is afoot, hopefulness returns, you adapt. You focus on the solution that is the most appropriate. You make up a game plan and a commitment to go along with it. You're off and running. You start to get excited about the new possibilities in your life. You begin to express from these possibilities.

Compared to the first three phases, *you're free*, baby bubba!

"Why not go out on a limb? Isn't that where the fruit is?"
—Frank Scully

It's Part of the Game

One of three things happens when humans are confronted by change: 1) we freeze up and bury ourselves in our habits, excuses or denials; 2) we try to skip the steps and grab the prize without paying the piper; or hopefully 3) we move through the four phases one-at-a-time in a congruent manner. If we stay in the *No Way* phase, we're asking for more trouble. The human system doesn't go well with denial. It breaks down and creates disease and other forms of distress. If we try to breeze through, we just elongate the process, and of course, this is just a subtler form of denial.

You have to allow the time it takes to plow through each phase. Change can be a demanding mistress, so don't add to the drama by judging yourself. Be gentle, be brave, the payoff is just over the next hill.

Also, facing change is endemic to the human condition. We all take a turn being the punching bag. Masters of change handle the forks in the road with as much grace as they can muster and they know the secret: you can't take it personally. It happens to all of us and the better you're able to view it that way, the easier it is to move through the phases and come out a more evolved person on the other side.

"If you have hope, you have help. If you lose hope, you will surely die—and death is final."

—Tony Magee, MS, MBA

Ha Ha Ha Healing

I know you've heard this saying before: "Laughter is the best medicine." Well, I can't say for certain that it's the *best* medicine, but it's certainly potent, and Norman Cousins' life is a great testimony to the healing power of laughter, and the critical difference that attitude makes.

Norman Cousins was born on June 24, 1915, in Union Hill, New Jersey. Growing up, he was both a fine athlete and a fine writer. He attended Teachers College at Columbia University and graduated in 1933. At this point, he began his career as writer and editor, starting first with the *New York Evening Post* and *Current History*. In 1940 he became executive editor of the *Saturday Review of Literature* (later *Saturday Review*). Two years later he became editor at the age of twenty-seven. Largely due to Mr. Cousins' stewardship, the circulation of this small literary magazine grew to over 600,000.

As influential as was his career—high among his chief concerns were world peace, justice and freedom—he will be equally remembered for the way he overcame two different life-threatening illnesses.

Upon returning from a trip to the Soviet Union in 1964, Cousins began experiencing stiffness in his limbs and nodules on his neck and hands. He was diagnosed with *ankylosing spondylitis*, a degenerative disease of the connective tissue, which causes the breakdown of collagen, the fibrous tissue that binds together the body's cells. When he began suffering adverse reactions to the medicine that he was administered, he decided to take matters into his own hands. He became determined to heal himself. He had read about the value of vitamin C and the power of attitude—positive emotions—so he checked into a hotel and, with the exception of intravenous injections of vitamin C, he discontinued his medications. Instead, he read humorous books and watched every funny film he could get his hands on.

He started this regimen almost completely paralyzed, but in time he experienced a gradual withdrawal of symptoms, and most of his freedom of movement. Over 3000 doctors sent him letters praising his decision to heal himself and supporting his mind-over-matter approach. As his condition improved, he went back to work at the *Saturday Review* and also wrote a book describing his dramatic healing adventure. *Anatomy of an Illness* may have inspired a humor therapy movement, but he wasn't quite finished offering living proof.

Fifteen years after overcoming *ankylosing spondylitis*, Cousins suffered a near-fatal heart attack while teaching in California. Again, he took matters into is own hands. He wouldn't take morphine, and he rescheduled visiting times so that he could get the rest he wanted. He gradually improved and chronicled his warm human story in a book: *The Healing Heart.*

Norman Cousins lived for another decade. We mostly remember him as the man who laughed his way to health, perhaps simplifying the self-healing method he developed. His contributions come to us in many forms. He spent his lifetime challenging the status quo. He led a hero's life. Awards included the United Nations Peace Medal, some fifty honorary doctorate degrees and he served as a diplomat during three presidential administrations.

The next time you find yourself in the middle of a deep-belly laugh, remember Norman Cousins. Because of his example, we know that laughter in not only fun, it's healing.

More than anything, Norman Cousins reminded us of the power of attitude. Your attitude is your constant companion. When it's shaky or dragging you down, remember Norman Cousins and have a laugh on him.

Thank you Norman.

"A merry heart doeth good like a medicine but a broken spirit drieth the bones."
—Proverbs 17:22

Now, to help you embrace change in your life, complete the following exercise and then read on.

LIFE-ESSENTIAL FOUR EXERCISE

Let's assume for a moment that you died painlessly and silently while reading this chapter. Now you're outside your body, looking down at it.

1. Are you proud of how you have been living your life?

2. What regrets do you have about your life?

3. Have you explored your natural talents, your gifts, by enthusiastically trying a variety of activities?

4. List your five major excuses for maintaining the status quo in your life. What would be the cost of ignoring each? Other than fear and cowardice, what stops you from risking change? Where can you buy the courage to overcome fear?

5. List five of the riskiest things you have ever tried. What were the consequences of each attempt?

6. List five times you took risks and the results came out worse than you had expected.

7. List five times you took risks and the results came out better than you had expected.

8. List five risks you would take now if the odds were better or the stakes worth gambling for.

9. Look over your lists. Do you see any patterns? If you aren't pleased with what you see, what changes do you want to make?

10. Ask the two people who know you best whether or not they think you are rationalizing away something you haven't the courage to do.

11. Now, if you were allowed to live again, how would you change your life?

LIFE-ESSENTIAL  5

POSITIVE THINKING VS. "STINKIN' THINKIN'"

Choosing a Positive Attitude

"To have 'good thoughts' is important, for a person becomes what he thinks. Gautama Buddha told us that. 'Mind is everything,' he said. 'We become what we think.'"

—Dr. Norman Vincent Peale

Most people don't cope with the world from a wheelchair or a hospital bed. Most of us are not overwhelmed with physical challenges, nor do we have to use a prosthetic to function. But it's often the case that people who experience such conditions maintain a more positive attitude than we do. This is possible when one has made the decision to focus on the winning factors inherent in their circumstances.

Rising to the Moment:
Kerri Strug & the 1996 Olympic Games

Few commitments in life are as challenging as training to be an Olympic athlete. Despite the gymnast's petite size, eighty-eight-pound, four-foot-nine-inch Kerri Strug had faced it all on her way to the 1996 Olympic Games in Atlanta—injuries, self-doubts, and a host of other setbacks. But there was one notion that she kept coming back to: *"A lot of times I thought about all the work I put into it, and I didn't want to blow it after I had gotten so close."*

At the 1992 Olympics, fourteen-year-old Kerri had been the youngest American rep for the U.S. team. In 1996, she returned at eighteen as one of the oldest U.S. gymnast team members. While she had trained over the years thinking an individual medal would secure her place in history, events turned in another direction. It would be the All-Around Team competition that would place Kerri in the history books.

During the women gymnasts' team competition, it appeared that the U.S. had the gold medal locked up. But then, Kerri's teammate Dominique Moceanu fell in not just one, but both of her vaults. Kerri would have to succeed with her second and last vault to help secure the medal against the Russians. The problem was that Kerri had ended her first attempt with a fall, and this had injured her ankle.

"Kerri, listen to me. You can do it," U.S. coach Bela Karolyi had urged. This was despite the fact that Kerri could hardly walk after the injury. Yet she would have to sprint down the runway, fling herself over the horse, and land gracefully on her good, uninjured leg!

Wanting to secure the gold for herself and the team, Kerri managed the vault on that day in July and assisted the U.S. in defeating the Russians. After her strong landing, Kerri collapsed in pain only to be picked up by coach Karolyi to collect the gold medal. It was later learned that Kerri had two torn ligaments and she was not able to go on into the individual competition at the Olympic Games.

But the vault had secured her fame. After winning the gold medal, Kerri and the other members of the U.S. women's gymnastics team were interviewed on lots of talk shows. She appeared with her teammates on Wheaties cereal packages. She also made it to the magazine covers of *Time* and *People,* and appeared on "Beverly Hills 90210" and "Saturday Night Live." All because Kerri chose a winning attitude that had kept her devoted to a gymnastic career since the age of five!

"When you do well, you think it's worth it. When you sacrifice so much and you finally do great, it feels sooooooooooo good."
—Kerri Strug

What Is Positive Thinking?

The dictionary defines the term attitude as *"a position of the body or manner of carrying oneself; a state of mind or feeling; disposition."* Another definition is: *"a mental set that causes one to react to a given stimulus in a characteristic and predictable manner."*

I was a sophomore at California State University, Northridge, when I first read *The Power of Positive Thinking* by Dr. Norman Vincent Peale. This book provided a deeper and more purposeful understanding of positive thinking. To this day, I still find myself reading it as one would read a book of Holy Scriptures.

What I learned from Dr. Peale was that one's present attitude is a result of one's present thoughts. On the surface, attitude is the way you communicate your mood to other people. When you're optimistic and anticipate successful encounters, you transmit a positive attitude and people usually respond favorably. When you're pessimistic and expect the worst, your attitude is negative and people tend to avoid you. Positive thinking is the way that you see things mentally.

"Whether you think you can or think you can't, you're right."
—Henry Ford

Your Attitude Is Your Choice

Albert Mensah, my good friend from Ghana, West Africa, is the author of *When the Drumbeat Changes; Dance a Different Dance.* At a business workshop in Dallas, Texas, Albert told a story about an African carpenter.

The carpenter had been building homes for thirty years. The time had come for him to retire. The carpenter went to his boss and announced: "Boss, today is the day I'm going to retire." The boss replied, "No, no, no you see, I have bad news and also good news." The carpenter wanted to hear the bad news first.

The boss told him: "The bad news is that I'm not going to let you retire. No, you can't retire today." The carpenter asked about the good news. "The good news is that we received a call last night from a man who wants to have a house built," the boss revealed. "It would be the most expensive house we've ever built. Since you're the best man for this job, can you please stay on and build this house?" Well, the old carpenter didn't want to do it. He had lost all his enthusiasm. He no longer had passion for his work. (My friend, the number one thing you must have is passion. Put some enthusiasm into whatever you do. In fact, you must become obsessed with it.)

The carpenter caved in and agreed to do the project. However, he built a lousy house. When the old man was done, he took the keys to the boss and said, "Boss, here are the keys to the house you asked me to build." And the boss responded, "Not so fast—*that house* is this company's gift to you."

The point is this! Our lives are our houses. If you build a lousy house, you get to stay in that house. If you build a better house, you get to live in that one. The attitude you choose is totally up to you.

"How you perceive experience and how you handle it determine how your life turns out in the long run."
—Bill Cosby

Window to the World

The house has four windows. The window on the north side has a view of a dull, drab gray building. When you look out that window, that's all you can see. The window on the east side looks out over an alleyway filled with trash and discarded junk. The window on the south side is boarded up. But the window on the west side has a most magnificent view of a wooded park with a grove of oak trees, a playground and happy, frolicking children. And in the late afternoon there is the most magnificent view of the sunset.

What window would you choose to look out of? Your attitude is like that window. You choose your attitude; it doesn't choose you. You either see opportunities or failures, possibilities or problems. Life presents the event; your attitude determines the experience. Two people with contrasting attitudes can participate in the exact same event and have totally different experiences. Two people go to the cinema and sit next to each other watching totally different movies.

We choose the window that determines our view of life. Excuse me for offering a cliché that we're all getting tired of: but is the glass *half empty* or *half full?*

Whatever you focus on expands. If your focus in life is on the problems, guaranteed, you're going to have problems. When you put your attention on the positive and let the negative fend for itself, not only do you create a better experience, you encourage more of the positive to come your way. Here's what I say: don't just focus on the positive, magnify it, exaggerate it, water it, let it bloom like a field of wild flowers! Hey, it's your life and at the end of the day, your attitude is the key to your enjoyment. The negative is out there, you don't have to go looking for it, but it's amazing how good life is if you choose a strong, positive attitude.

"You are what you think you are all day long."
—Ralph Waldo Emerson

Be the Torch

Years ago I read some great advice. I don't remember the source. When you turn on a light in a room already lit, you make the room a little brighter, but when you turn on a light in a totally dark room, you make a major difference. The whole room lights up. The shadows disappear, the ominous becomes commonplace, solutions and possibilities pop up all over the place.

Nice thought, but I say take it even further. Carry your blazing torch with you wherever you go. Be the torch. Like darkness, negativity has no station in the splendor of illumination. One person with an authentic, consistently positive attitude can create an unbelievable impact. No question about it, we're surrounded by negativity. Glance at the front page of the daily newspaper, listen to the chitchat at work, talk to the neighbors, there's a lot of fear hidden behind masks of negativity. You don't have to buy into it. Be the torch. Stay positive. Light up the night! If it weren't for the dark, light wouldn't have much to do.

What do you want in your life? If it's impact and results, be the torch. If it's joy and happiness, be the torch. If it's contribution, BE THE TORCH! Your attitude is the difference.

"Sometimes our light goes out but is blown into flame by an encounter with another human being. Each of us owes the deepest thanks to those who have rekindled this inner light"
—Albert Schweitzer

You Will Produce What You Constantly See

Throughout life, certain elements of our overall environment will bombard us with negative thoughts. There will be thoughts of failure, poverty, defeat, depression, can't do it, don't have what it takes, and on and on. If we make the mistake of dwelling on these kinds of thoughts, before long, we'll start seeing ourselves all defeated and depressed. Somehow, we have to protect our mind from this junk. We cannot afford to let stinkin' thinkin' control our lives. No one can control your thought-life for you. You have got to be diligent and stand guard over the doorway of your own mind.

When thoughts of defeat, depression, and poverty come to your mind; don't give them the time of day. Immediately, cast those thoughts out—don't even give them five seconds of your thought-time. Wrong thoughts create the wrong images. Right images will lead you down the right path. If you have negative images in your mind today, the good news is that they don't have to stay there. Remember, we have to learn how to replace those negative thoughts with good ones.

I heard an interesting story about a young lady named Tara Dawn Holland. From the time she was a little girl, Tara had a dream to become Miss America. In 1994, Tara entered into the Miss Florida contest and won the first runner-up position. So she decided to try again the next year. Tara entered the same contest, and once again, she won the first runner-up designation. She was tempted to get down and discouraged, but Tara didn't do that—she stayed focused on her goal. Tara decided that a change in environment was needed, and she moved to Kansas. In 1996,

Tara entered the Miss Kansas contest—and believe it or not she won! Later on that same year, Tara went on to be crowned the new Miss America. Tara saw her dream come to life at last.

People talked to Tara after the contest was over; many asked about the secret to her success. The new Miss America told how after losing twice in a row, she thought about giving up. But Tara didn't do that. Instead, she went out and rented every video of every pageant that she could get her hands on. She studied the local pageants, state pageants, Miss Teen, Miss Universe, Miss World—whatever she could find. In all, Tara rented over 500 videos of various pageants, which she watched over and over again. Tara told how every time she watched them, she pictured herself in the winning situation. She pictured herself receiving the crown and walking down the runway in victory. Time and time again, Tara envisioned herself winning. A reporter asked Tara if she was nervous walking down the runway in front of millions of people on television as the announcer belted out the famous Miss America song. Tara replied, "You see, I wasn't nervous at all. I had walked down that runway thousands of times before."

Now my friend, let me ask you—have you ever walked down that runway before? Have you ever seen yourself accomplishing your dreams? Do you keep that vision of victory in front of you? Tara Dawn Holland had realized that she could never be a winner until she saw herself as a winner. She had to get rid of those thoughts of losing. Tara had to destroy that negative image that was telling her she was going to be runner-up once again. She had to develop a "can do" attitude. Tara saw herself stepping onto the winner's platform. She saw herself walking down that runway in victory. She created an environment of faith and success. What you keep before your eyes will greatly affect you. You're going to produce what you continually see.

"Every thought is a seed. If you plant crab apples, don't count on harvesting Golden Delicious."
    —Bill Meyer

Catch Fish? No Problem!

A man was fishing along the seashore. He had no problem catching fish that day. He would catch really big ones—as long as three feet—and then throw them back in. The smaller ones he would keep. Another fisherman noticed that the man had been doing this all day long, so he had to walk over to the man and ask him about this behavior. "Pardon me, my good man," the fisherman said, "I don't mean to be nosy—but I couldn't help but notice that you have been tossing back your big fish and keeping the smaller ones. Sir, why are you doing this?"

The man replied, "Because I only have a ten-inch frying pan."

The man's attitude was centered on that ten-inch frying pan, so he was limited to the smaller fish. The ten-inch frying pan was all that he had ever used. It was all his father had ever used and his grandfather as well.

How many people do you know who desire big things to come into their life—such as a job promotion, a dream home, a business loan, an audition, or a new relationship—and then the moment that they get it, they don't quite know what to do with it. So they blow their great opportunity! They tend to mess things up because all that they have ever known is their small way of thinking.

"Ev'ry day fishin' day, but no ev'ry day catch fish."
—A Bahamian Proverb

Whose Clothes are you Wearing, Whose Thoughts are you Thinking?

"Here Sonny-boy, take my clothes. They were good enough for me, they were good enough for my daddy, they're good enough for you." With that, the father gave his son the clothes he expected him to wear the rest of his life. Sonny—loyal child that he was—didn't question this gesture. He just put the clothes on and wore them out in the world. It didn't matter that the clothes were out-of-date and not really his own. It didn't matter that they didn't come close to fitting. He simply did as he was told.

Until one day he saw a shirt that he liked, so he bought

it. He didn't want to dishonor his father's legacy, so he put the new shirt on over his father's frayed shirt. Of course, he looked ridiculous. Even more ridiculous when he bought a pair of pants that appealed to him and he wore them over his father's baggy slacks.

It's much the same with the thoughts we carry around in our heads. Others gave us most of these thoughts, especially the people influencing us in our early years. Mommy, Daddy, Uncle Harry, Sister Regina—and of course, the generous media. Television, radio, newspapers and magazines are oh-so-willing to fill us with group thought so we don't really have to do any of our own thinking. So much of our negative thinking is handed down to us like old clothes. We don't know better, so we put them on and make do.

It doesn't work. You have to get rid of the old clothes before you can replace them with clothes of your own choosing. The scruffy shoes, the baggy pants, the torn shirts, the battered hat—they have to go!

You can't just put these clothes in the back of your closet and go about your merry way. These clothes have had too much influence in your life to give it up now. Before long, you'll get the idea that the old hat goes pretty well with your new outfit—even if it is an embarrassing misfit. Here's what you do: create a ceremonial fire and burn every piece of your dad's hand-me-downs. Otherwise, before long, you'll be wearing the whole outfit and not really know why.

Burn your old clothes and buy brand, spanking new ones—that you picked out, that fit your lifestyle and represent your tastes, values and aspirations.

In other words, let go of the beliefs, opinions and judgments that you inherited from your upbringing. Clear your head of these cobwebs and fill your mind with the freshest, edgiest thinking you can muster.

And when you have kids of your own, burn your old clothes before you're tempted to pass them on.

"The people you allow to embrace your life ultimately have the greatest impact on your attitude."
—Keith D. Harrell

Windshields & Rear-view Mirrors

When people drive automobiles, they are usually focused on moving their vehicle in a forward direction. They spend most of their time looking through the huge front windshield of their car or truck. Every once in a while, they briefly glance up at the rear-view mirror to evaluate the situation behind them. They do the same for their side-view mirrors—to switch lanes or to see who's coming up along-side. We should remember to approach life in a similar fashion. We should spend most of our time focusing on the windshield of our lives, and simply glance at the side and rear-view mirrors when necessary. Your bright future lies through the large windshield, which is ahead of you; through the small rear-view mirror lies your past, which is definitely behind you.

The Three R's

In Chapter One, I mentioned when we were younger, the 3 R's stood for *readin', ritin',* and *rithmetic.* (Obviously, whoever thought this up was an atrocious speller.) Now that we're adults and know how to read and rite and have calculators to do all our 'rithmetic, I offer an improved version of the Three R's for choosing a positive mental attitude: Respect—for self and others, Responsibility—for all our actions, and Risk—because nothing worthwhile happens without taking a risk!

"You are today where your thoughts have brought you. You will be tomorrow where your thoughts take you."
—James Allen

If I Had a Hammer!

There once was a young boy who had a bad temper. His dad gave him a bag of nails and told the boy that every time he lost his temper, he must hammer a nail into the back of the fence. Over the next few weeks, as the boy learned to control his anger, the number of nails hammered daily gradually dwindled down. He discovered that it was much easier to hold his temper than to drive those nails into the fence!

Finally, the day came when the boy didn't lose his temper at all. He told his dad about it and the father suggested that the boy now pull out one nail for each day that he was able to hold his temper. The days passed and the young boy was finally able to tell his father that all the nails were gone.

The dad took his son by the hand and led him to the fence. He said, *"You have done well, my son, but look at the holes in that fence. The fence will never be the same. When you say things in anger, they leave a scar just like this one. You can put a knife in a person and draw it out. It won't matter how many times you apologize, the wound is still there. A verbal wound is as bad as a physical one. Friends are very rare jewels indeed. They make you smile and encourage you to succeed. They lend an ear, share words of praise and always want to open their hearts to us."*

"How we think shows through in how we act. Attitudes are mirrors of the mind. They reflect our thinking."
—David Joseph Schwartz

Polishing Up Your Attitude

We can keep our attitude on the sunny side by applying the following adjustment techniques. They can help you keep hold of your great attitude or repair it if need be. Everything we do is affected directly or indirectly by our attitudes. A change in a person's attitude can have an effect on just about everything else in that person's life. Even a small sway in attitude adjustment can have a profound effect on what we do and how we do it.

Protect Yourself from Negativity: We all know that it's ludicrous to think we can get rid of every single negative factor in our lives. We all must learn to deal with things that do not quite go our way. Nearly everyone has gone through a time when they had to share space with a difficult relative, co-worker, boss, classmate or roommate. And other people have managed to maintain their positive thinking in the face of a truly challenging family issue that challenges any resolution. By hook or by crook, they find ways to handle it all in a positive manner in spite of the seemingly-permanent negative situation. By all means possible, work to insulate your attitude against the negative factors you face. When negative energies are in your environment, use the following techniques to help shield yourself from harm's way:

1. Change your surroundings.

2. Laugh it off.

3. Speak it out.

4. Disclose your issue to the Divine.

5. Work through it.

Out of Sight, Out of Mind: I've always maintained that people's lives and minds are just like their closets and garages. If their closets (and garages) were truly organized, their thinking would be too. Many people unconsciously clutter their lives with negative factors, which make it difficult for them to be positive. They seem to surround themselves with unnecessary problems, which produce more possessions, commitments, and relationships. Then they whine about the difficulties within their lives. The solution to this madness is simple. Free yourself from complications. Practice the "out of sight, out of mind" attitude adjustment method. When your mind is not cluttered, life's smallest rewards seem more abundant and enjoyable. As the best-selling author Dr. Richard Carlson says, *"If you don't sweat the small stuff, it won't hold you down."*

Focus on Your Strengths: In business marketing, marketers usually pour additional advertising dollars into their "hottest product." Their philosophy is: *"Don't waste time and money trying to promote the weaker products—just focus on the stronger ones that make us our profits."* You can use this same belief, which can help you adjust and maintain a more positive mental attitude. You definitely have special strengths in your life. The more you focus on them, the better you'll become.

Flip the Script: The main key element that differentiates *positive thinking from "stinkin' thinkin'"* is a good sense of humor. A well-developed sense of humor increases one's ability to develop a positive mental attitude. Some folks just "flip the script" to turn the situation around and enhance a sense of humor. Whenever something negative occurs, they immediately find whatever humor is present within the circumstance. This allows them to minimize any negative impact the incident may have on an otherwise wonderfully positive mind-set.

Have a Sense of Direction in Life: People who know where they are going in life, usually have better attitudes than those who don't. You can just about tell when folks have a sense of direction and purpose—just by the way they walk and talk. When they walk, their heads are usually held high, smiles on their faces, *pep in their steps*. When they speak, their words are carefully selected and their comments almost always have a positive twist. Having a mission in life provides direction. It allows for better focus, drives away fears, offers perspective, and wipes out uncertainty.

Improve Your Self-Image: There was a television commercial in which a very attractive young woman approached a handsome, well-groomed young man in a room full of people. From her viewpoint, everything about this guy was wonderful. She walked right up to the guy and gave him her best pearly-white-teeth smile. When he smiled back at her, his teeth were *butter yellow.* With great disappointment, the lady quickly made a cool U-turn and disappeared into the crowd. (It was an advertisement for a new whitening toothpaste from Arm & Hammer.)

Self-improvement of any kind should be applauded, but the overriding reason for improving your self-image is to look better to yourself, not to please others. You should always look your best. When you improve your appearance, you give your positive attitude a large boost.

Increase Your Physical Workout: Jackie knows what a difference working out can make. Not only has it helped her lose inches and pounds, but it also helped her get through some troubled times. "I was bound and determined to get my life back," says Jackie, who usually works out at the Spectrum Health Club in West Hills, California. "As I worked out and lost weight, I felt better and better about myself. It kept me strong—both emotionally and physically." Jackie has put her energy into participating in the L.A. Marathons and AIDS Walk L.A. She finished a sponsored bike ride for AIDS research—from San Francisco to Los Angeles. "I don't know what my life would be like if I didn't work out," she says. Jackie hopes others will be inspired by her example. Many fitness buffs depend upon working out to keep themselves out of a "stinkin' way of thinkin'."

Keep Your Positive Attitude by Giving It Away: Sometimes you run into people who really *get on your last nerve*. These folks inspire such remarks as: *"I really can't stand him!" "She's a huge pain in the 'you know what!'"* Or *"Oh no, not that crab!"* When you are irritated by the behavior of others, it can be easy to *"tell 'em off"* or *"give 'em a piece of your mind!"* Give 'em a piece of your mind, but instead of giving them a negative piece—give them a slab of your positive attitude. Keith Harrell, author of *Attitude Is Everything™*, once told me, *"Tony, just kill 'em with kindness!"* When you choose to give your positive attitude to others, it creates a relationship of two or more different organisms in a close association that may benefit each person involved. At the end of the exchange, everyone feels much better. The greatest secret is this—you keep your positive attitude by giving it to others you come in contact with.

"Oliver Wendell Holmes once attended a meeting in which he was the shortest man present. 'Dr. Holmes,' quipped a friend, 'I should think you'd feel rather small among us big fellows.' 'I do,' retorted Holmes. 'I feel like a dime among a lot of pennies.'"
   —Oliver Wendell Holmes

Grace + Attitude = Gratitude

"Grace: a) unmerited divine assistance given man for his regeneration or sanctification b) the quality or state of being considerate or thoughtful."
—Webster's New World Dictionary

The real power behind positive thinking can be attributed to two important words: grace and attitude. Put them together and you have the formula for harmonious living: Gratitude. As my personal friend, the great teacher of life and public speaker Zig Ziglar says, *"The more you are thankful for what you have, the more you will have to be thankful for."*

If you're serious about winning in life, be grateful for the opportunity to simply exist as a human being. Be thankful for every little thing you have in life. Wake up thanking God for your unconquerable soul. Start your every day with a sense of gratitude, and then spread that gratitude around like a bee spreads pollen.

GRACE + ATTITUDE = GRATITUDE

The best way to express your gratitude is to heap praise on all corners of your personal universe. Praise is the action of gratitude. Tell the people in your life—your mate, your children, your parents, your friends, your fellow workers, your boss—what you sincerely appreciate about them. Don't hold back. If you're new to the gratitude game, like anything else, it takes practice, but once you get the hang of it, you'll never go back to the old, hidden, noncommittal way of being.

An attitude of gratitude not only makes the people in your life feel better, it ensures that you're going to have more and more of what you really want. There is a great principle at play here. *Whatever you focus on you increase.* When you practice praising the folks you come in contact with, you create an environment in your world that all-but-guarantees success. Give it your all. Repaint the world with all the vibrant colors of your grace and appreciation. Dr. Norman Vincent Peale once said,

"Whatever you are doing, give it all you've got. Give every bit of yourself. Hold nothing back. Life cannot deny itself to the person who gives life his all."

Here's my challenge to you. Find someone in your life who deserves your praise today—and give it to 'em!

"Develop an attitude of gratitude, and give thanks for everything that happens to you, knowing that every step forward is a step toward achieving something bigger and better than your current situation."

—Brian Tracy

How Many Fingers Do You See?

In *Patch Adams* (a movie with Robin Williams in the lead role that tells of the story of an extraordinary medical doctor), there was an old business executive who had been committed to an insane asylum. The old man walked around the ward holding up four fingers, asking each person he encountered: "How many fingers do you see?" Everybody would say, "four," and in response, with a hard frown on his face the old man kept repeating the number four, "FOUR-FOUR-FOUR-FOUR!" Over and over, all throughout the movie, this scenario was replayed.

Finally, toward the end of the movie, the old man talked to Dr. Adams. Holding up four fingers, the executive once again asked, "How many fingers do you see?" Like the others, Patch Adams replied, "four." The old man angrily said, "Patch you're not looking! How many fingers do you see?" He told Patch Adams to look past the hand—beyond the fingers. And when Patch focused past the hand—like an optical illusion—the four fingers became eight. Robin Williams said, "Wait, I see eight fingers." Softly the old man murmured, "Good... good... " When we look past what we obviously see—we see so much more. Joy is the ability to look past what obstacles that are before you.

There is joy in a positive attitude. Joy is the ability to handle your present—whatever it may be—based on what is waiting in the future. There are too many folks today who cannot take much! As soon as a storm rises, they start shivering and give up. The strong winds of *Problemsville* start blowing in their direction, and they are ready to throw in the towel. Listen, if you can't take it—you won't make it! In this life we all gotta go through some stuff! Plus, there will be people who won't like it when you try your best to be your best. There are some who don't want to see you blessed! You must look right past folks like that, because there is joy for you on the other side—trust me.

"Man's mind, stretched to a new idea, never goes back to its original dimensions."
    —Oliver Wendell Holmes

If by Rudyard Kipling

If you can keep your head when all about you
Are losing theirs and blaming it on you,
If you can trust yourself when all men doubt you,
But make allowances for their doubting too;
If you can wait and not be tired by waiting,
Or being lied about, don't deal in lies,
Or being hated, don't give way to hating,
And yet don't look too good, nor talk too wise:

If you can dream and not make dreams your master;
If you can think – and not make thoughts your aim;
If you can meet with Triumph and Disaster
And treat those two imposters just the same;
If you can bear to hear the truth you've spoken
Twisted by knaves to make a trap for fools,
Or watch the things you gave your life to, broken,
And stoop and build 'em up with worn-out tools:

If you can make one heap of all your winnings
And risk it on one turn of pitch-and-toss,
And lose, and start again at your beginnings
And never breathe a word about your loss;
If you can force your heart and nerve and sinew
To serve your turn long after they are gone,

And so hold on when there is nothing in you
Except the Will, which says to them: "Hold on!"

If you can talk with crowds and keep your virtue,
Or walk with Kings—nor lose the common touch,
If neither foes nor loving friends can hurt you;
If all men count with you, but none too much;
If you can fill the unforgiving minute
With sixty seconds' worth of distance run,
Yours is the Earth and everything that's in it,
And—which is more—you'll be a Man, my son!

—Rudyard Kipling

Since your mind can hold only one thought at a time, make each thought you hold constructive and positive. Look for the best in people and ideas. Be constantly alert for new ideas that you can put to use in your life.

And lastly, treat all of us as if we are your very wealthy relatives who have placed you in our wills to inherit $30 million. Start this habit and practice it consistently. If you do this—you'll benefit from it for the rest of your days.

"It's not what happens to you, but how you react to it that matters."
—Epictetus

LIFE-ESSENTIAL FIVE EXERCISE

1. Examine and write down your attitude towards yourself and other people. How do you feel in regards to success, freedom, work or school, and your life in general?

2. What are some specific ways in which your attitude toward your loved ones (your circle of family and friends) could become better?

3. What are some specific ways in which your attitude toward your co-workers and others you frequently run into could become better?

4. Create a list of improvement-goals for your positive mental attitude.

LIFE-ESSENTIAL  6

THE CHICKEN IS INVOLVED; THE COW IS COMMITTED

Setting Goals & Achieving Them

*"For the most part, people generally don't have problems achieving
  their goals; they have trouble setting them."*
    —Zig Ziglar

Dr. Conwell & the Acres of Diamonds

Russell Herman Conwell was born in 1843. He would live to
inspire the lives of millions of people worldwide. Russell
Conwell practiced law, was a journalist, and a theologian. He is
famous for a speech titled "Acres of Diamonds." The crux of this
speech is that opportunity awaits us ubiquitously and is always
available. Numerous accounts suggest that Dr. Conwell's lecture
was delivered over 6,000 times—all across America. This speech
helped Dr. Conwell to raise millions of dollars; with the money,
he founded Temple University—located in Philadelphia,
Pennsylvania—for deserving young Americans. Many business
experts believe that this story helped to create the system of free
enterprise in the United States.

Dr. Conwell once traveled down the Tigris and Euphrates Rivers with a party of Englishmen; the group's tour guide was Arabian. The guide did more than just lead their journey; he kindly entertained the tourists with the most interesting stories. The following tale particularly stayed with Dr. Conwell.

Not far from the River Indus, there once lived an ancient Persian fellow by the name of Ali Hafed. This man owned a very large farm that had orchards, grain fields, and gardens. All he had on his mind was somehow amassing large amounts of wealth.

One day, an old Buddhist sage visited Ali Hafed and told him, "A diamond is a solid drop of sunlight." Ali heard all about diamonds, including how much they were worth, and suddenly he felt poorer than he had been prior to hearing about such precious gems. The farmer was poorer because he was unhappy. He also feared being poor one day. He wanted a mine of diamonds for his security and lay awake all night dreaming about it.

Early the very next day, Ali sought out the old Buddhist wise man to question him. He asked the sage: "Where can I find these diamonds of which you speak? I wish to be exceedingly rich." The sage told Ali that if he could find a river that ran through white sands, there he would find diamonds. The wise man told Ali that there were plenty of such places—all he would have to do is to go and find them.

With hopes of pursuing his dreams, Ali Hafed sold the farm, collected his money, and went off in search of diamonds. He began his search at the Mountains of the Moon. Thereafter, he moved out into Palestine, then strolled on into Europe. Eventually, his money was depleted and Ali was miserable, and raggedy. In this state of scarcity, he stood on the shoreline of a cove at Barcelona, Spain. When a great tidal wave came rolling in between the pillars of Hercules, the poor, troubled, tormented, failing man could not resist the awful temptation to throw himself into that incoming tide. Ali Hafed sank underneath its foaming top, never to be seen again.

One day, the man who had purchased Ali Hafed's farm led his camel into the garden to drink. As the camel put its nose into the shallow water of the brook, Ali Hafed's successor noticed a peculiar burst of light from the white sands of the watercourse. He pulled out a black stone with an eye of light that reflected all the colors of the rainbow. He took the small rock into the house and put it on the mantel, which covered the fireplace. Then he forgot all about it!

A few days later, the same old Buddhist priest came in to visit Ali Hafed's successor. The moment he opened the door the holy man saw that flash of light on the mantel. The priest rushed up to it, and shouted: "Here's a diamond! Has Ali Hafed returned?" "Oh no, Ali Hafed never returned," the new farmer replied impatiently, "and that is not a diamond. That is nothing but a stone I found in my own garden." "I tell you I know a diamond when I see it," said the priest. "I know positively that this is a diamond."

Together, Ali's successor and the old sage rushed out into that old garden and stirred up the white sands with their fingers: Behold!—they came up with even more beautiful and valuable stones than the first!

The moral is clear: If only Mr. Ali Hafed had taken the time to carefully prepare himself—to gain knowledge of what diamonds looked like in their rough state—all of his wildest dreams would have been his reality. Ali would have recognized that what he desired was right at home the entire time.

The reason this story had such an overwhelming effect on Dr. Conwell and later, on millions of others, was the thought that each and every one of us is, at this instant, standing in the center of his or her own acres of diamonds!

And what about the acres of diamonds around you?

Have you explored the many opportunities within your immediate surroundings? Remember this: setting and achieving your goals may only be accomplished with sound objectives supported by sound plans. Regardless of what goal you seek, the very thing you're doing at the present could possibly establish the road to it.

"Before we go running off to what we think are greener pastures, let's make sure that our own is not just as green or, perhaps, even greener. It's been said that if the other person's pasture appears to be greener than ours, it's quite possible that it's getting better care. Besides, while we're looking at other pastures, other people are looking at ours!"

—Earl Nightingale

What's Your Life Strategy?

Here's another important question for you. Would you catch an airplane flight without knowing its destination? No!, and why would you? Usually there is a specific purpose for traveling, with a set goal in mind. Goals set our direction, identify opportunities, improve working relationships, and establish targets to be aimed at. Goals offer the motivation necessary for growth and success in important areas of almost every aspect of life.

What's your life strategy? As I stated in Chapter Two, you must live your life intentionally—on purpose. In pursuit of a great life, you must have a strategic intent. By strategic intent, we refer to the purpose(s) a person or organization has and the ends being pursued. This can be very broadly based (vision and mission) or more focused (goals and objectives). For example, at the broadest level, your personal intentions may include a vision of a long, happy, fulfilling life, but you may also have a much narrower expectation of making an A grade in a particular course. Typically, in order to reach your broader expectations, you must first achieve a series of narrower ones; therefore, it's important that you align your broad and narrow intentions. If you are not careful, you may invest time, energy, and other resources in reaching narrow objectives that don't move you closer to your broader vision.

The hierarchy of strategic intent includes five types of elements: (1) a *broad vision* of what or where you should be in life, (2) your *mission*, (3) *specific goals*, (4) a breakdown of the specific goals into various strategic *objectives,* and (5) specific *plans* for accomplishing each objective.

Strategic Intent

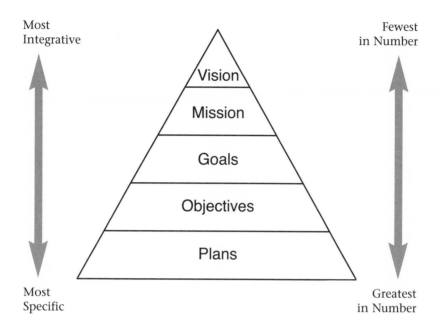

Let's take a closer look at each of these elements.

A *vision* statement represents your aspirations for the future, without specifying the means that will be used to achieve those desired results. It also describes what position you want for your life over a given period of time.

A *mission* statement documents the purpose for your existence and directly ties into your vision.

Goals are open-ended statements about desirable outcomes, such as, "losing weight," "getting out of debt," or "going back to school and earning a college degree." These are specific actions to be achieved.

Objectives, on the other hand, are more specific and, as a consequence, are measurable tactics that you will use to reach and attain goals. "Losing fifty pounds in six months," "paying off the balances of three high-interest credit cards by next year," or "taking two courses per quarter for the next two years" are all tangible, measurable statements about desired strategic outcomes.

The lowest level in the hierarchy of strategic intent deals with the *plans* that you must develop to help accomplish your objectives.

"Goals are not only absolutely necessary to motivate us. They are essential to really keep us alive."
    —Dr. Robert Schuller

If You Think It, You Should Ink It

A goal (the main subject of this chapter) is an end toward which you direct some specific effort. It is an accomplishment to be achieved with measurable objectives and plans. Goals must include factors of time and cost considerations. Any goal— which is not written in ink—is in jeopardy. If you *think it*, you should *ink it*. Larrie Rouillard, author of *Goals and Goal Setting*, teaches us that writing our goals in "black and white" gives us more explicit statements of our intentions and the results we want to reach.

Daydreaming about our goals is not enough. By writing down our goals, we can make sure we're including all the necessary elements. It's actually the first of several commitments we shall make to ourselves to reach our goal.

Your goals cannot be achieved without personal commitment and effort. For the most part, there must be motivation. Motivation is the key to forming a commitment to do whatever is needed to reach your goal and fulfill your mission, which supports the vision for your life.

HUMAN BEING + MOTIVATION = COMMITMENT

"Everyone in the world is motivated to do exactly what they are doing right now; whether it's working on their life's dream or sitting on the couch at home in the middle of the day working on that third bowl of cereal watching Ricki Lake."
    —John W. Alston

The Pro from Prague

Martina Navratilova was born in Prague, Czechoslovakia, in October 1956. Arguably the greatest tennis player of all-time, Martina revolutionized women's tennis with her superb athleticism and raised the sport to an entirely new level.

By the time she retired in 1994, Martina had amassed a staggering number of records, including 168 pro singles titles, breaking Chris Evert's previous record of 157. Martina set a new record with nine Wimbledon championships. She also holds 165 doubles titles. She has earned more than $20 million in prize money. She won eighteen Grand Slam Singles titles, including her record nine Wimbledon crowns, four US Opens, three Australian Opens and two French Opens. Martina is a true testament to setting and attaining real goals.

During her magnificent professional tennis career, a sports reporter interviewed Martina Navratilova after one of her wins at Wimbledon. Full of admiration for the tennis genius, the reporter said to Martina, "My, my, my, Martina... no one can deny that you are surely involved with this game." Martina said kindly, "What do you mean, Sir? I'm not involved; I'm committed!" The sports broadcaster then asked her what the difference was. Martina replied, "There's a big difference between being involved and being committed. The difference is like a plate of steak and eggs; the chicken is involved, but the cow is committed."

Our Father Knew Best

Venus and Serena Williams—the dynamic duo of professional tennis today—set out to become the greatest athletes in this chosen field of sports. The tennis phenoms were born in Lynwood, California, in 1980 and 1981 respectively. Together these siblings are taking the tennis world by storm.

Venus and Serena grew up in Compton, California—a gang-plagued city outside Los Angeles. In the early years, their father Richard Williams saw a tennis player earn a prize of $30,000 after winning a tournament. At that very moment, Richard had a dream to develop his two youngest daughters into tennis champions. The only real obstacle in his way was not knowing much about playing the sport. Richard taught himself by studying an instructional video.

As soon as Venus and Serena were old enough to properly hold a racket, he began teaching them all he had learned. They practiced daily with countless dead tennis balls near their home, in an environment that featured drive-by-shootings and drug dealers hanging around the cracked-surface tennis courts.

When Venus was ten, and the girls were already winning tournaments, the Williams family moved to Palm Beach Gardens, Florida to further pursue their dad's vision. In 1991, Rick Macci, who coached Monica Seles and Andre Agassi, began to train the two future stars. Soon, however, Richard Williams took over all aspects of coaching and marketing for both extraordinary daughters.

Richard was involved in every aspect of his daughters' lives. He even pulled the sisters from middle school in Delray Beach, Florida to be taught at home. Having a great education was a cardinal principle in the formula for their success. He would cut back their tennis tournaments whenever either sister's grades dropped below an A.

In 1999, Venus defended the Lipton title, defeating her younger sister Serena in the final match to become the first sister duo to meet in a WTA Tour Final. En route to that final match-up, Venus beat No. four Jana Novotna and No. seven Steffi Graf, ending Graf's twenty-one-match Lipton winning streak.

In the same season, Serena, seeded seventh, upset No. one Martina Hingis, No. two Lindsay Davenport, and No. four Monica Seles on the way to her first career Grand Slam singles title at the US Open. Thus Serena became the lowest seed to win the women's title since 1968, the sixth American woman to win in thirty-one years, and the second black woman ever to win a Grand Slam singles title. (Harlem's Althea Gibson had won five, her last coming at the 1958 US Championships). After the Open, Serena's ranking moved up to a then-career high No. four. And when Serena won the French Open doubles title with her sister Venus, they became the first sisters to win a Grand Slam crown together in the 20th century. By 2002, the Williams Sisters were worth well over $200 million combined, with cash prizes and major athletic endorsements. As of this writing, Venus is the highest paid female athlete from a single endorsement: $40 million over five years with Reebok.

After years of being whipped by her older sister on the tennis courts, Serena has arrived. Public opinion about which of the Williams sisters is the better player shifted from Venus to Serena after the younger Serena easily defeated her older sister Venus in the Finals of the 2002 US Open, 6-4, 6-3. This produced the third straight Grand Slam title for Serena—and she had defeated her sibling each time. Ranked No. one in the world in 2003, Serena defended her crown—defeating sixth-ranked Jennifer Capriati at the NASDAQ Open in New York.

Nevertheless, these two sisters are both No.one in my book. I believe neither sister would be tops in the world without each other.

Do Your Goals Pass the T.O.N.Y. Test?

Chances are, you know a thing or two about goals. You've read the quotes and statistics lauding the power of goal-setting. Maybe you've had a fling or two at stating your goals, but it didn't work out. Here's the thing: writing down your goals and hoping they will magically change your life is a formula for failure, not success. Your goals have to meet certain criteria, or they're not really achievable.

I want you to succeed, and goals are a critical part of your success strategy. With this in mind, I have devised a simple acronym to insure that your goal-setting has the best chance of success. I call it the TONY Test. (All right, you caught me. Now, every time you think about a new goal you'll also think about me, but what's so wrong with that?)

T.O.N.Y. stands for *Tangible... Obtainable... Nameable...* and *Yours.*

T   Tangible

O   Obtainable

N   Nameable

Y   Yours

Tangible... Is it quantifiable? Can you measure it? Will you know when you've accomplished it? If not, then it's not really tangible, so head back to the drawing board. Losing a few pounds someday is not a tangible goal.

Obtainable... Can you actually achieve this goal, or is it a pipe dream? If you're a five-foot-three inch couch potato and you set a goal to play in the NBA, you've just set yourself up for failure and frustration.

Nameable... Is it specific? Can you clearly define it? Wanting to be a better person is not a nameable goal because it's not specific enough. Exactly, what would it look like if you were a better person? You have to spell out the details of the goal.

Yours... Is this something you really want, or is it something that others want for you? Just as important: *why* do you want it? There is a world of difference between wanting something in order to make a fellow worker jealous, as opposed to wanting something because it will upgrade your career, or your health and well being. Your true intention behind your goals is the key to your motivation. Our goals motivate us when they're in line with deep purpose.

When you're setting your goals, keep TONY in mind. Set goals that are clearly defined, that stretch you out but are still possible for you to reach, that can be measured, and most of all, set goals that inspire you. Goals are meant to spur you to action and if they pass the TONY Test, they should.

The Goal Ghouls

Of course, there are two parts to the Goal Game. First, you set goals that pass the TONY Test. Secondly, you create a game plan that streamlines your follow-through.

Here's the simplest, most effective goal plan that I know of: rewrite your goals every morning, and read them out loud four times during your day. Period. Don't miss a day. What are your goals for this day? How are you going to meet them?

Know this, there will be challenges. I call them *Goal Ghouls*. Physical, emotional, psychological obstacles will pop up to challenge you on your destined path. Don't try to sweep these good-for-nothings under the carpet; they won't stay there.

Instead, (1) identify them as clearly as you can, then (2) create a plan to overcome them.

Don't make this complicated. If your goal has passed the TONY Test, in almost all cases, the obstacles that show up are just part of the process. Denial is the enemy here. When the princess was able to call out Rumplestilskin's name, he lost his power. The same is true with the blocks in the way. Identify them and immediately go on to the solutions.

The masters in our midst don't skirt the problems. They see them for what they are, and then they focus on solving them.

Two Goal Killers

The two most common—and most dangerous—obstacles to goal achievement are *procrastination* and attending to *unproductive activities*. The late George L. Graziadio (whose name was chosen for the School of Business and Management at Pepperdine University), shed light on the procrastination issue in a commencement address he gave to the MBA Fall Class of 2000. He said the best way to defeat the procrastination syndrome is to use the "T-N-T" method: do it "today, not tomorrow." Procrastination is putting off until "tomorrow" what could be done "today." You can also avoid procrastination by:

1. Attaining enough *motivation* and *inspiration* to achieve the goal.

2. Setting clear *priorities* for important tasks.

3. Breaking needed tasks into *smaller components*.

4. Setting *small deadlines* for each task.

5. *Rewarding* yourself when tasks are over and done with.

Engaging in *unproductive activities* may cause your personal energy level to deplete. You may find yourself getting irritated for wasting your valuable time on such unfruitful events. If someone asks you to participate in some task that does not add value to your life or personal situation, learn to just say no. We must avoid as many non-productive activities surrounding our lives as possible.

"Procrastination is the art of keeping up with yesterday."
   —Don Marquis

3Ws + 2Hs = Goal Achievement

There are three actionable elements that ensure goal achievement: *Execution, Examining,* and *Improvement.* When planning your goals, it's easier to take action when you ask yourself the following questions—*Who, what, when, how and how much?*—on a periodic basis.

- **Who** is assigned the responsibility for coordinating the activities needed?

- **What** is to be accomplished?

- **When** must the activity be completed?

- **How** will the goal be achieved and what obstacles could hinder your progress?

- **How** much will this cost in dollars, resources, and personal time?

Along the way, remember that goals cannot be achieved merely through planning and simply being eager. Action must be taken. Your goals need to be executed—then carefully examined, and improved upon.

"A 10,000 miles journey starts with the first step."
   —Ancient Chinese Proverb

Don't Stop 'Til You Get Enough

Examining reviews the progress you're making toward the goal. It compares your plan with the actual results. The use of quantifiable expected developments and specific milestone dates can be helpful. When change is needed, consider improving your objectives and tactics. Look at what is working and what isn't. Only employ the tactics that work and draw you closer to your goal. Usually you won't be improving the goal; instead you'll change only the means to achieving the goal. The combined examining and constant improvements will allow you to be more productive. You shall continue until your goal is achieved. As Michael Jackson, the King of Pop Music, once sang, *"Keep on with the force, don't stop—don't stop 'til you get enough!"*

According to the "acres of diamonds" principle, everything we could ever hope for is probably very close at hand; we have the talent, abilities, education, and backgrounds to realize our ambitions right in our own surroundings.

Now, to help you set and achieve your personal goals, complete the following exercise and then continue on to Chapter Seven.

LIFE-ESSENTIAL SIX EXERCISES

1. Write your major goal in life.

2. List five benefits that you will enjoy as the result of achieving your major goal.

3. What is your present status?

4. When are you going to achieve your major goal?

5. List five obstacles you will have to overcome to reach your major goal.

6. What knowledge will you have to gain to finish your goal?

7. Identify at least five people and two organizations whose assistance you will need to accomplish your goal.

LIFE-ESSENTIAL 7

NOT BROKE; JUST OVERCOMIN' A CASH FLOW CHALLENGE

Having Financial Discipline

"You must learn how to use your money more effectively, else your money will end up using you."

—Ping Jeng Long

Taking control of your financial situation—the very sound of it delivers a shiver of self-confidence. Once you're in control of your money, you can then do what is necessary to achieve your most important financial goals. However, you should not be in a rush. A lot of individuals incorrectly think that the way to become financially independent is to jump into the world of stocks or mutual funds and hope to pick some sure things. Becoming knowledgeable in every area of your personal finances is the real secret to financial freedom. By making the right money moves within each component—from debt reduction to a solid savings plan to estate planning to proper tax preparation—will set you up for financial success.

At present, you'll need to know exactly where you stand with your money before taking any steps toward improving your financial destiny. By putting down on paper the actual numbers representing your finances—your assets, your liabilities, and your net worth—you'll see where you need to start working. After you have organized and evaluated your own money, you can treat yourself to an eye-opening experience. Later in this chapter, you'll see a chart displaying items you might purchase that contribute to your net worth – and those that do not. I also provide you a worksheet that will show you how to calculate your net worth. Financially, it is important that everyone knows his or her net worth status at all times.

I'll Take the Million, Mr. Thomas

Mr. Frank Thomas—my Kenyan-born fifth grade teacher from Lexington Elementary School, in Pomona, California—once asked our class this question: *If a person offered you a million dollars in cash today versus a penny whose current value would double every day for one month, which of the two offers would you accept?*

With almost zero delay, all the pupils in the entire class responded loudly. The unanimous answer was something like: "Shucks, that's easy Mr. Thomas. I'll take the million dollars!" "Are you sure?" he asked. My classmates responded with comments like: "Yeah, we're sure." "Wouldn't you?" "You've got to be crazy not to take that much money." Mr. Thomas looked over to my area of the classroom and called me up to the front of the class. "MAGEE (that's what everyone called me since there were two of us named Tony), GET UP HERE!" I was a bit nervous—because when he called me up to the front, he sounded mad. We all know how excited teachers can be at times when they really want to make an important point.

Mr. Thomas handed me a big, fat calculator and instructed me to enter the following: 0.01 (which is equal to one cent). Then he said, "Multiply it by two." The result I got was 0.02 or two cents. He then said, "Multiply that answer by two, and then the next answer by two, and then the next, until you've done this thirty-one times. (Representing the thirty-one days). By the time I had finished multiplying, the amount had grown to $21,474,836.48. Your eyes aren't deceiving you: over $21 million accrued in only one month, compared to the $1 million chump change that we all had accepted so blindly. Sure, we were a bunch of ten-year-olds without a handle on the meaning of money, but Mr. Thomas had planted a seed in us all—an important lesson in finance that would serve us for a lifetime. Have patience and discipline, and be smart with your money.

"Money is the manifestation of power."
　　—S. E. Anderson

Your Dollars: An Immediate & Longer-Term Resource

Each dollar comes into our lives for a purpose and for a period of time. We decide which of our dollars to spend right away and which ones to save for longer-term goals. Longer-term goals include saving for college, raising the down payment on a house, or investing for retirement. Once a dollar is spent, it is gone forever—like a season that has passed. Consequently, it's important to do everything to hold on to a portion of your earnings.

Understanding how dollars can be used as immediate or longer-term resources is important. This is significant because *only funds invested for the long term can help you increase your net worth.* Here's a basic guideline: invest your dollars for five-year terms or even longer ones. The following table lays out common immediate and longer- term goals. It will help you understand the difference between the two and their impact on your net worth.

"Without money, you have no control. Without control, you have no power."
　　—Spike Lee

Immediate & Longer-Term Goals

Immediate Goals	Contribution to Net Worth
Car lease	no
Clothing	no
Credit cards	no
Entertainment	no
Gifts	no
Groceries	no
Term Insurance	no
Travel	no
Other Current Expenses	no

Longer-Term Goals	Contribution to Net Worth
Art collectibles	yes
Automobile payments	yes
Business ownership	yes
House payments	yes
Investments	yes
Retirement plans	yes
Whole life insurance	yes

Undisciplined Spending

As you see above, most of the dollars that undisciplined spenders earn remain in their possession for only a short period of time. This time frame may be hours, days, or weeks depending upon the due dates for their monthly bills. Therefore, such people never benefit from having longer-term investments. The so called "trappings of financial achievement"—clothing, expensive cars, electronic equipment, household gadgets, fine wine, etc. can hinder undisciplined spenders. They tend to invest in the trappings of financial achievement—rather than the real substance of success—investments that build their net worth.

Many of us spend our hard-earned dollars on things we really can't afford. For example, someone might purchase a $1,000 watch—just to tell the time—versus a nice $85 Fossil timepiece. Someone else might buy a $500 Gucci pocketbook, or a Louis Vuitton, or Dooney & Burke,—and yet carry only five dollars in it. If we think about it, some of our financial decisions and upside-down priorities don't even make good nonsense!

No matter how old you are or how much money you make, you'll want to zero in now on the key financial goals you hope to achieve. Too often, people just have vague notions about what they want financially. They have goals like: "I don't want to die broke," "I want to be at ease," or "I want stocks that will go up." Their goals are indefinite. Trouble is, these goals are too nebulous to give you much.

Instead, you ought to become more precise and decide exactly what it is you want to have and when you want to have it! For example, your goal might be. "I want to retire at age forty-five instead of sixty-five with a quality of life greater than before retirement," "I want to pay cash for a brand new Lexus ES400," or "I want to have enough money saved to travel and tour Germany, Italy, Africa, and Tierra del Fuego."

The best way to make the right goals is to figure out *what's important*, and *what isn't*, and *when* you want to achieve your goals. Once you've placed priorities on your financial goals, you can adopt appropriate strategies to hit your financial targets. It's crucial to divide your goals into short, medium, and long-term commitments.

"Don't buy no $85,000 car—before you buy a house."
—E-40, Popular Hip-Hop Recording Artist and Actor

Our Attitudes & Prosperity

Dr. Creflo A. Dollar, Jr.—a popular clergyman who ministers out of College Park, Georgia—explains the true meaning of prosperity in his eye-opening series *The Intangibles of Wealth*. Dr. Dollar also discusses how to change our attitudes in order to position ourselves to receive abundance via spirituality. His message: our *attitudes* about money will determine our *altitudes* in relation to it.

Dr. Dollar clearly states that money is not the problem; it's the person with—or without it. Here's the problem with too many of us: we're interested in the fruit, but we ignore the root. Dr. Dollar says that if you sow a seed in the soil, the life of that seed is going to start in the roots. You can't see this—you only see what eventually comes up above the surface. But if you don't invest in what you *can't see*, you'll never get a tree that produces fruit-bearing branches.

We're interested in the fruit, but we ignore the root. The root of prosperity is your attitude. You cannot prosper until you realize that you've got an attitude stopping your prosperity. This conversation is not about getting rich today, then ending-up broke tomorrow. This conversation is about working on the root so that it will bare fruit every season.

Prosperity is not about getting some of it now, only to not have it later. Prosperity springs from a perpetual state of well-being—and this is everyone's right. It's an inward attitude. Prosperity also equals charity, which simply means *giving from you to someone else—using the extra fruit to cause a blessing in someone else's life*. Prosperity in your life is not just about money; it's also about healing, family, society, health, benevolence, and peace of mind.

Once the root goes down in the ground—and is established—once the seed starts growing and coming up, then I mean to tell you that the fruit from the tree may be used to go out and bless humanity.

Let's slow down here. Before we discuss financial planning, let us entertain two important ideas: *What does it mean to be rich?* and *What is debt?*.

"When you can count your money, you ain't got none."

—Don King

What Does "Being Rich" Mean?

Some people dream about the lifestyles of rich celebrities and successful entrepreneurs. They wonder what it must be like to live in mansions, travel in private jets, and have other folks pay their debts. At the same time, for the majority of us, the idea of being rich is plainly a castle-in-the-sky and not the kind of life we really think we can achieve.

We wonder what it really means to be rich. So many of us equate wealth with having a certain amount of ready cash, say—$1 million, $10 million, or $100 million at our disposal. Obviously, this varies from individual to individual. Interestingly, even people we think are rich—because they have these cash reserves—may not feel *rich enough*. For instance, someone might be jealous of his neighbor with the brand-new drop-top Bentley. In spite of that, the Bentley owner is envious of the couple living in the beautiful mansion down the street.

Now and then, I get into debates over the importance of money. More than once I've heard the argument, "I don't really want to be rich, I just want to be comfortable." I must say I don't feel that way. Over the years, I've learned that in order to *be comfortable, you have to be rich.*

In a conversation with Les Brown, "The Motivator" and world-renown Hall of Fame speaker, I mentioned that I had then recently completed my MBA from Pepperdine University. He happily replied, "That's a tremendous accomplishment. Congratulations Brother." Then he added, "I have an MBA too." "But Les," I replied, "You said you didn't have a college education." Les shot back, "Tony, you're right. The MBA I have is a Mega Bank Account!"

Now that I think about it, I should have asked Les if he wanted to trade MBAs!

Bottom line: People should learn to respect money and understand that money is not the root of all evil. (If anything is the root of evil, it's the *lack* of money.)

Most people think that being rich is to never be troubled about money, to live with comfort, to have enough for your children's college tuition, with enough surplus to help them out with a down payment on a vehicle or home. Being rich means not worrying about where the next paycheck is coming from or how to pay for that gift for a dear friend. For most people, to be truly rich is to be financially unconstrained and to have the ability to live life in a comfortable manner.

What we perceive as being rich will naturally change over the course of our lives. A thirty-year-old generally has a very different idea about what being rich means than a fifty-year-old.

At age thirty, being rich might mean being able to pay

off all those college loans and high interest credit card balances—with enough left over for a down payment on a new home. At age fifty, rich might mean having the time and money to travel, to stroll the shopping mall on a weekday, to golf when you want to, and to know that a comfortable retirement is not far off.

"You will hear people say, 'Money won't bring happiness.' The earning and possession of money has brought a lot more happiness than poverty has. Money is a warm home and healthy children; it's birthday presents and a college education; it's a trip abroad and the means to help older people and the less fortunate."
—Earl Nightingale

What Is Debt?

Okay, now that we have a good handle on what "being rich" might mean, let's look at the opposing question, "What is debt?"

Basically debt is:

1. Any service you take without paying for it when you receive it.

2. Any amount of cash you borrow without collateral.

3. Any credit extended to you.

Here are some common ways debt is incurred:

• You purchase a thirty-two-inch television from Circuit City—and charge it.

• You don't have the money for a new suit of clothes, so you call your grandparents for help.

• You pay for lunch with your American Express or Visa card.

• You're in need of immediate dental assistance

(two fillings and a bridge), but you're broke. You have to arrange a payment plan with your dentist.

- You need $1,000 to tide you over for a month, so you go to the bank for a signature loan.

- You're a little short on funds this week, so you tap a friend at work for $50.

- You need your tax refund now, so you ask your cousin for $200.

- Your day-care payment is due, so you request a deferment from the provider or an advance on salary.

- You use your Chevron charge card to gas up your vehicle.

- You fly with your buddies to Cancun, Mexico for your spring vacation and put the tickets on your United Airlines charge account.

In all of these examples, you've gone into debt. You owe money to other people. These lenders have no collateral from you—your dentist can't re-sell the materials used on your mouth and Circuit City can't convert your promise to pay into immediate cash.

Now, it's your turn. Take a few minutes for self-discovery. On a pad of paper, write down the ways you've gone into debt over the past twelve months. Use any of the above examples that are true for you.

When done, draw a line beneath that list. Now make a second list. Include any other ways in the last year you've incurred debt that weren't mentioned in the first list. Be creative.

Finally, make a third list; focus here on all the ways you've noticed that your friends incur debt. Take a really good look at these three lists. They're a lot longer than you would have thought, aren't they? And they all add up to the same thing... you guessed it—debt.

"The best thing you can do for poor folks—is not to be one."
—Rev. Ike

What's Your Net Worth?

To substantially increase your net worth, you'll need to identify the financial resources you have to invest. Therefore it is imperative that you understand which dollars you want to *spend* and which ones you wish to *invest*. Adopting a long-term investment philosophy can be difficult. Staying focused on your long-term goals is a big challenge. One of the best tools to help you stay focused is a financial plan.

We all need some type of financial system to keep our personal finances under control. The system should consist of four elements: (1) controlling expenses; (2) paying bills; (3) establishing a savings program; and (4) keeping records for tax and other purposes.

The first step in getting organized is to fill out a personal balance sheet that lists your assets and liabilities. In this way you can determine your net worth, which is an accurate indicator of your financial health, and the base from which you can make all future money decisions (such as setting saving and spending goals). In figuring out your net worth, your assets will consist of personal property, jewelry, art and other collectibles, stocks and bonds, insurance, and annuities. Your liabilities consist of all current unpaid bills. For loans, count only the principle due on your car, education, and other loans, not the interest. Your lender can give you these figures if you don't know them. You should determine your net worth once a year to measure how much it has grown or decreased.

Date _____

Assets

Cash and Investments

    Checking accounts   _____

    Savings accounts   _____

    Money market funds   _____

    Outstanding loans

      (to others)   _____

    Bonds   _____

    Stocks   _____

    Certificates of deposit   _____

    Treasury bills   _____

    Retirement accounts:

    IRAs and Keoghs   _____

    Gold, silver, platinum

      (at today's value)   _____

    Cash value of insurance

    and annuities   _____

    Profit-sharing plans   _____

    Real estate   _____

    Other   _____

Total Cash and Investments $_____

Personal Property

    Car   _____

    House   _____

    Furniture   _____

    Jewelry, antiques,

    art, furniture   _____

    Other   _____

Total Personal Property $_____

TOTAL ASSETS $_____

Liabilities

Current Bills

Mortgage or rent	_____
Utilities	_____
Taxes	_____
Charge account balances	_____
Insurance premiums	_____
Medical	_____
Furniture	_____
Other	_____

Total Bills $_____

Loans

Home mortgage	_____
Education	_____
Car	_____
Loans against life insurance	_____
Other	_____

Total Loans $_____

TOTAL LIABILITIES $_____

Total Assets $_____

minus **Total Liabilities** $_____

NET WORTH $_____

Are you excited by what you see or, are alarms going off in your head? Remember, the best time to start "moving on up" (like George and Weezie from the 1970s television sitcom *The Jeffersons*) is today. It's never too late. If your total puts a grin on your face—stay on course!

"To some, money might not be the most important thing in our society, but to many others, it's right up there with oxygen."
—Rita Davenport

Hey, Where'd All My Money Go So Fast?

Financial control consists of 1) learning how we spend our money and then 2) *changing these patterns* to suit our goals. Sounds simple, doesn't it? While it's not always easy, self-awareness is key. Your goals should include saving for both short and long-term plans and having sufficient cash to cover unexpected expenditures. To determine the amount you normally pay out for food, entertainment, or other categories, keep a record of your spending in a notebook for one month and then supplement this information with your checking account records.

When you create an expense record, it will serve as a snapshot of your current budget. It reflects the personal choices you've been making. For instance, your housing costs may be on the high side and your transportation costs minimal because you've chosen to spend more on rent or live in an urban area close to your office. By living in the city rather than in a suburb, you might be able to walk or take a bus to work, eliminating the cost of an automobile. Remember, geography plays a huge part in your budget. Items such as housing and entertainment will be higher if you live in Los Angeles, California than in Oak Ridge, Tennessee.

Establishing a Savings Program

"In God we trust, all others pay cash."
—Anonymous

Now that you know where your money has been going, let's consider what you should be saving. Why bother to save, you ask? One reason is that overspending leads to a dangerous cycle. With no savings, unforeseen needs will force you to borrow money at high interest rates, pushing you further and further into debt.

Setting aside a fixed amount each month is the best way to develop sound financial discipline. There is a basic money principle that applies to everyone regardless of marital status or financial situation: pay yourself first. This means set aside money from every paycheck for savings and investing, even if it's only $50.

A worthy goal is at least 10 percent of your gross pay. For instance, say you earn $50,000 per year and take home $35,000. Savings of $5,000 to $6,500 per year is a good target. If hefty education debts make the goal unattainable, then aim for 5 to 8 percent of your gross income. The amount you set aside is not as important as learning to save a fixed amount on a regular basis, at least in the beginning years of financial independence.

You've Got to Pay Your Bills

Establishing a bill-paying schedule is an important step in a personal financial system. The best method is to choose one convenient time each month for paying all the bills. Most creditors will allow you to change the due date of your bill if you ask. That way, all your bills will be due around the same time.

You may want to schedule your bill-paying system to maximize the time it takes for a check to clear your bank and be deducted from your account. If your money is in an interest-bearing checking account—and it should be—it will earn interest until the time the check clears. This is called "float time." Here are three easy ways to squeeze the most "float" out of your dollars:

1. Pay your bills just before their due date, not the minute you receive them or beyond the due date. (Chronic lateness in bill paying will damage your credit report.)

2. When given the choice of paying by check or credit card, responsibly use the credit card. The monthly billing cycle means your money will stay in your checking account longer. Note: If you won't have the money in your checking account to cover the purchase when the bill arrives, don't buy it now with the credit card.

3. Pay late in the week or just before holidays. Creditors usually do not process payments over the weekend or during holidays where usually the offices are closed for business. This may buy you additional float time.

It will also be helpful to keep a list of all your regular monthly bills you have each month. This list could be kept in the computer or on a legal pad. This will help you avoid over-looking a payment if a bill gets lost in the mail. Check the bills you have against the list each month.

Being the Cheerful Giver

"When someone gives the hospital a gift of $5 and you know he can afford less than that, thank him graciously. When someone gives the hospital $5,000 and you know he could afford five times that, say, "that will help."

—Robert H. Thorson

Anyone can afford to give, no matter what his or her condition. It's only the belief that you are unable that prevents you from being charitable. If you don't have $1,000 to give, you have $100. If you don't have $100, you have $50. If not $50, then give $20, if not $20, then $5. If not $5, then give a dollar or ten cents. The point is: give something! If you don't give money, give of yourself: listen to a friend who needs a good ear, tutor, mentor, get involved in community service, perform whatever deed that appeals to you.

Why should we give? Simply said, developing a capacity to give helps tear down the distorted idea that we don't have anything to offer—that there's so little for us that we can't afford to give any of it away. It also can help prevent the anger behind the old belief that life or other people are somehow responsible for our situations and that we're helpless to change things. By giving, we begin to see abundance. The Bible says it, *"The more ye giveth—freely and without resentment, for the sheer sake of giving— the more ye shall receive."*

There's a biblical principle called "tithing," which means to donate at least one-tenth of your earnings or belongings to charity. Consider this an option. Whether it is your holy place of worship, a scholarship fund, or a favorite nonprofit organization, it can be motivating to give ten percent of your net income to charity in the name of the Creator who made your one hundred percent possible! You still have ninety percent left over to work with.

"Give, and it will be given to you... For by your standard of measure, it will be measured to you in return."
—Luke 6:38

Five Helpful Hints To Becoming Debt-Free

1. Create a spending plan.

2. Make paying off debt a top priority.

3. Cut back on your spending and all credit card use.

4. Watch for impulse buying.

5. Seek professional advice from a debt counselor.

Life-Essential Seven Exercise

You can better understand your financial situation by completing the following:

1. What is your present net worth?

2. Set financial goals for yourself. What would you like your net worth to be:

   In 5 years? $_____

   In 10 years? $_____

   In 20 years? $_____

3. How much money do you want, specifically? How much do you need in order to live in the way that you want to live?

   There are three amounts of money that you should decide upon: (1) the yearly income you want to earn now or in the near future; (2) the amount of money you want to have in a savings and/or investment account; and (3) the amount you want as retirement income.

   Set your financial goals.

   Yearly income:

   Financial reserves:

   Retirement income:

4. Who in your line of work is presently earning that amount of money? If you know of somebody at that level, you'll know what you'll have to do to earn it.

5. Continue to make plans for increasing your service to others, for making yourself more valuable. The money will follow!

LIFE-ESSENTIAL 8

PIGEONS & EAGLES
Competent Leadership

"Asking 'Who ought to be the boss?' is like asking 'Who ought to be the tenor in the quartet?' Obviously, the man who can sing tenor."

—Henry Ford

Leader of the Flying Red-Tailed Airmen

African-American pioneer Benjamin Oliver Davis, Jr. competently led the famed Tuskegee Airmen. One of the first African-Americans to graduate from West Point in the 20th century, he was turned down for pilot training in 1936. In 1940, he was finally accepted to pilot school. Quickly, because of the war and his skill, Davis was promoted to Lt. Colonel and given command of the 99th fighter squadron. Later he was promoted to Colonel and was given the 332nd fighter group. While under his command, the 332nd never lost a bomber on an escort mission. They also received a Distinguished Unit Citation. After World War II, Davis became the first African-American Air Force General. Benjamin O. Davis, Jr. is an American hero. He's also a great example of a very competent leader.

In thinking about leadership, two important aspects need to be considered: (1) how being a leader compares to being a manager and (2) what traits are characteristic of the best leaders. This chapter will explore these topics. As you read, consider how the ideas presented are reflected in your own life and your own leadership qualities. We can all be leaders, even if we don't know it yet!

"The first responsibility of a leader is to define reality. The last is to say thank you. In between, the leader is a servant."
—Max DePree

Under The Influence

When I was first working as an engineer, scientist, and business strategist for The Boeing Company in Southern California, I didn't notice any similarities between leaders and managers. Maybe this is because their likenesses are like a narrow stream of water, whereas their differences are as wide as the Gulf of Mexico. Leadership emphasizes the general influence process, whereas management traditionally focuses on the activities of planning, organizing, staffing, and controlling. *Influence* is what defines leadership. All of us can exercise a certain degree of influence on someone, at some point, in some place. Leadership isn't about titles, positions, or flowcharts. It's about one life influencing another.

Leaders and Managers Aren't Synonymous

Do leadership and management really differ? I would argue that there are far more real differences than distinct similarities between the two occupations. Grace Murray Hopper, Retired Admiral of the U.S. Navy said, *"You manage things; you lead people."*

A basic difference between managers and leaders is attitude. Attitude is everything. Many managers are content to set modest goals, to pacify others, to try for a comfortable working environment, and to use power cautiously. A leader tends to set more demanding goals, to challenge others, and to create a more dynamic working environment.

While some overlap can definitely be found between management and leadership, a closer look shows that they are vastly different. A good manager is content to simply follow directions and suggestions from higher bosses. A leader is more apt to consider the future, anticipating needs and issues before being told that action is needed. A good manager is willing to accept responsibility; a leader seeks responsibility. An effective manager will take modest risks—mainly when the odds are favorable. A leader accepts higher risks when they have the potential to result in greater progress, and he or she commits to a plan of action with greater determination. A leader has more of an "entrepreneurial spirit" than a basic manager.

A manager seems to be more apt to accept comfortable assignments, while a leader looks for more demanding opportunities to demonstrate leadership potential. A manager usually views those under his or her supervision as employees. A leader views employees as team members and followers.

"People don't want to be managed, organized, stereotyped, tagged or filed. That's what you do with things in an office. People are dynamic and must be led through love and relationship."
—John C. Maxwell

Are You a Leader or a Manager?

There is a world of difference between leading and managing. Managers are obsessed with keeping things in order, and being consistent. Managers make sure that nothing falls out of the box. They plan, they budget, they organize, they solve problems, and they meet, and meet, and meet.

Conversely, leaders are focused on vision, vision, vision. Leaders want to keep the action moving. They're great communicators and motivators, inspiring the forces towards the vision. They're not concerned with the box. If thinking has to happen outside the box to fulfill the vision, so be it.

Abraham Zaleznik, a Harvard Business School professor, argues that a crucial difference between managers and leaders lies in the conceptions they hold—deep in their psyches—of chaos and order. Zaleznik says that leaders tolerate chaos and lack of structure and are thus prepared to keep answers in suspense, avoiding premature closure on important issues. The professor states that, in contrast, managers seek order and control, and they are almost compulsively addicted to disposing of problems even before they understand their potential significance!

It's important to acknowledge that leadership at any level is built on basic management skills. Until an operation is well managed, the person in charge is not sufficiently free to lead. Thus those attempting to lead without fundamental management competencies usually fail before they get started. Some would argue that one could not effectively lead an organization while constantly putting out fires. Managers who desire to lead must free themselves by learning to be: (1) superior teachers, counselors, and delegators; (2) outstanding time managers who are good at setting priorities and establishing goals; and lastly, (3) excellent system and control developers and operators.

"The man who wants to lead the orchestra must turn his back on the crowd."

—James Crook

Pigeons & Eagles

In the community surrounding the Nickerson Gardens Housing Project (where I lived as a child), the one bird that could be found anywhere you looked was the pigeon. They were so abundant that many of the young boys in the neighborhood would capture them and keep them in homemade coups as pets. The boys would train the pigeons to follow simple commands. To this day, catching pigeons is a favorite pastime of many young boys at the hard-up Nickerson's Project.

The pigeons were relatively easy to capture. They would congregate in large groups in open areas of my neighborhood and usually fly no higher than the two-story apartment buildings we all lived in. It seemed that they would only use their wings to fly back and forth from the ground to the rooftop.

Pigeons aren't hunters; they're beggars. You could feed them just about anything, and they would chow it down. They are also scavengers. Pigeons are commonly found at places where there is an abundance of rubbish to be picked over. Basically, they eat just about anything not nailed down. And soon afterwards, they "handle their nasty business" all over the place—on park statues, cars, porches, walkways—and even on the heads of some of us.

Even though they were fun pets in the projects, I wouldn't consider pigeons to be an admired bird amongst most people in the world. They are certainly not the most intelligent birds that God has to offer.

On the other hand, let's examine the brilliant bald eagle. While I was a graduate student at Lehigh University (a school built on a mountainside in Bethlehem, Pennsylvania), I saw the majestic bald eagle for the very first time. The sight was incredible. The eagle was alone and flying high, in clear view, moving with amazing grace in large circles through the sky, more than likely surveying the land for a source of food.

Although the eagle is a physically strong bird with a wingspan up to twelve feet, this bird's most remarkable feature is its *eyesight*. To survive, an eagle must be able to see, from very high altitudes, squirrels, field mice, rabbits and other rodents on the land, and salmon, sea bass, and other fish swimming near the surface of the water. The eagle's astonishing eyes are large, second only to its beak as the animal's primary facial feature. The eagle's extraordinary vision allows it to enjoy a quality of life that pigeons could live only in dreams.

The difference between the pigeon and the eagle is this—the pigeon has sight, but the eagle has vision.

"The most pathetic person in the world is someone who has sight but has no vision."
—Helen Keller

Soft Traits Are Often Overlooked

In looking for the right leader to take an organization to its full potential, many companies focus only on the technical background and relevant experience of a potential candidate. Too often, they don't recognize the "soft traits" that identify a great executive. You see, executives are hired based on technical traits, but they're usually fired because of the wrong combination of "soft traits"—the human characteristics. The essential elements of these "soft traits" include honesty and integrity, intellectual capacity, intensity, leadership, and passion.

Author Stephen Covey tells us that effective leaders are well-principled people. They build a deep level of trust in organizations in a short period of time, and this trust is a key precursor to driving change in these organizations. They ask people to take significant risks with many unknowns. Therefore, a deep level of trust is needed for the organization to succeed. The effective executive's honesty includes self-appraisal—knowing where he or she is strong as well as what abilities need improvement.

Outstanding leaders are smart. They can distill a complex situation down to actionable components and understand the dynamic of multi-track environments while working well within them. In newer situations, they quickly soak up the relevant information and ask questions for clarification. These leaders are not embarrassed by what they don't know—instead they eagerly seek to understand.

Exceptional leaders have a track record of delivering extraordinary results. They have a personal work ethic that inspires and drives teams to succeed. They can tell you how they accomplished goals. They have focused energy and intensity, but are not simply known as workaholics. Their careers encompass new and increasing challenges that may include setbacks, but not failure. Their enthusiasm is infectious and helps to create a positive feedback loop in the organization—that in turn draws in other great people.

Many books have been written on leadership, but what are the key elements? In my course of study, I learned that they involve developing a *unique culture* and possessing strong *decision-making* abilities. The leader sets the tone for an organization, making it a place where followers can grow and be challenged. The best leaders subscribe to the belief that leadership is a demonstration of power acquired, not invoked. In making decisions, they have a balanced sense of risk and confidence. They have thought over the consequences so that when mistakes are made, the organization can easily recover from them.

Brilliant leaders know that what they do makes a difference. This is the reason they get up in the morning to put in that long day. Personal passion is the bedrock on which their other traits are built. I have learned that having the right combination of leadership traits and knowledge is rare, but essential. The leaders that possess these skills are in high demand because they make an impact on organizations that goes well beyond their immediate scope of influence.

"Being in power is like being a lady. If you have to tell people you are, you aren't."

—Margaret Thatcher

An Officer and a Gentleman

"If you think something is wrong, speak up. Bad news isn't wine. It doesn't improve with age."

—General Colin Powell speaking to his officers

A study of leadership could not be complete without including one of the great heroes of our time: General Colin Powell. During my graduate trek at Lehigh University, I had the pleasure of meeting and spending some valuable time with General Powell—now our 65th Secretary of State. He may describe himself as a fiscal conservative with a social conscience, but to millions of Americans, he is a true military hero and one of the most admired men in our country.

To me, he is the quintessential leader.

Colin Luther Powell was born in Harlem in 1937 and was raised in the South Bronx. His parents, Luther and Maud Powell, immigrated to the United States from Jamaica. They instilled in their son a deep sense of old-fashioned values. Secretary Powell was educated in New York City public schools, graduating from the City College of New York (CCNY), where he earned a bachelor's degree in geology. It was there that he found his calling when he joined the Reserve Officers Training Corps (ROTC). He graduated in 1958 at the top of his class with the rank of cadet colonel, the highest rank in the corps.

Powell was one of the 16,000 military advisers dispatched to South Vietnam by President Kennedy in 1962. A year later he was wounded by a punji-stick booby trap and was awarded the Purple Heart. Later he would receive the Bronze Star, and during his second tour of Vietnam, he received the Soldier's Medal for rescuing his comrades from a burning helicopter, despite being injured in the crash himself.

All told, Secretary Powell would receive eleven decorations, including the Legion of Merit.

Throughout his entire life, Colin Powell has displayed solid and unwavering leadership qualities. His propensity for hard work and respect for God and country moved him swiftly through the ranks. Moreover, he has always shown a high regard for family, demonstrated most notably by his devotion to his wife Alma and their three children.

Secretary Powell was a professional soldier for thirty-five years, holding various positions of leadership, eventually rising to the rank of Four-Star General. He earned a reputation for mental toughness in Vietnam, Lebanon, Grenada, Panama and in Kuwait during Operation Desert Shield. One writer likened Secretary Powell's life to other leaders who demonstrated unselfish service in their time: General Ulysses S. Grant, Benjamin Franklin, and Booker T. Washington.

As I write about Colin L. Powell, I am most impressed, not with his formidable achievements, but with his down-to-earth leadership style. He has a keen, self effacing sense of humor, unusual in a leader of his magnitude. He doesn't really fit the typical profile. For example, when he was named commander over 75,000 American troops in Germany—the V Corps—he gave his seniors officers great latitude when it came to making decisions, and he invited openness, even disagreement and criticism. He told them that sharing a problem with the boss would not be "seen as weakness or failure, but as a sign of mutual confidence." He assured them that he wanted their honest opinion, that he considered it a mark of loyalty to be straight with him, even if he didn't like what they had to say. At the same time, once a decision was made, the debate was finished. "From this point on, loyalty means executing the decision as if it were your own."

General Powell assured his men (and women) that he

didn't hold grudges. If a mistake was made, he expected his people to acknowledge it and to do better next time. If one of his directives wasn't clear, he wanted to be asked for clarity, and if the second or third explanation still didn't cut it, he would assume that the problem was with the transmitter not the receiver.

One of the most noteworthy parts of Colin Powell's leadership style is the atmosphere that he creates. He has always encouraged his officers to have fun in their commands and to make sure that their families didn't suffer. He has said, "I don't intend to work on weekends unless it's absolutely necessary, and I don't expect you to do it either."

I think Colin Powell is a great example for all of us because his leadership has always been grounded in respect. He respects the men and women he works with, and he stands behind them. He vows to do everything to help them perform their missions. Too often, this critical element is missing in our leaders. Instead, a sense of competition and "mistake-counting" prevails.

In his last assignment, General Powell was the twelfth Chairman of the Joint Chiefs of Staff, the highest military position in the Department of Defense. During his four years, he oversaw twenty-eight crises, including Desert Shield and Desert Storm operations. He retired from the military in 1993 and returned to private life. He wrote his uplifting autobiography, *My American Journey*, which was published in 1995. In it, he enumerates the lessons he has learned from the heroes in his life. He also began a public speaking career, inspiring audiences both in the US and abroad.

Upon his retirement from the military, he was urged to run for public office but he declined. Instead, he focused on young people as the chairman of *America's Promise—The Alliance for Youth*, a national nonprofit organization dedicated to building the character and competence of young people.

In 2001, President George W. Bush appointed Colin L. Powell Secretary of State, the first African-American to hold this office. Since taking office he has played a leading role in rallying America's allies and the United Nations to the war against terrorism.

To me, the mark of great leaders is their ability to hold

the vision within an atmosphere of openness. When people know that they aren't being held up to a standard of unobtainable perfection, and that their opinions will be heard and honored, agendas move forward. This is Colin Powell's way.

"A good leader is a guy who can step on your toes without messing up your shine."
—Anonymous

I Can See Clearly Now

Effective leaders generate excitement, interest, and energy in others. And they do this primarily through effective communication. How leaders talk about their visions determine whether others will want to mentally "sign-up" with them.

A major key that effective leaders use in speaking about vision is consistency. Effective leaders are usually eager to describe their vision in rather predictable ways. This is not because they lack creativity. It is because their vision does not change from day-to-day. Leaders focus on how the future will look as a result of their vision. They describe the benefits inherent in their vision and their personal belief in its importance. A vision declaration is not a set speech given from notes at formal occasions. Rather, it appears to be impromptu and delivered to anyone who will listen. If you want others to follow you, you have to get out there and describe where you are going. The consistency becomes important so that others will get a clear picture of where you are taking them. Sometimes managers find communicating a vision difficult. For them it's more comfortable to stay in the office and do a job. This is not leadership.

Repetition is the other part of effective communication. Speaking a message only once is not enough. An effective leader's messages must be continuous and repetitive. At first, followers will wonder if the leader is serious or "is this just the flavor of the month?" After people hear the message frequently enough and see that the leader's behaviors are consistent with the message, then, and only then, will they begin to believe. When followers know leaders are determined, they fall in line with the leader's vision.

Leadership Qualities

Communication rides high on a leader's must list, but it's not the only skill required to get the job done. Patricia Guggenheimer and Mary Diane Szulc, authors of *Understanding Leadership Competencies*, conducted research among leaders from corporate, private, government, community, and education sectors. The following are the characteristics that well-rounded, impactful leaders must possess.

Courage

Creativity

Enthusiasm

Humor

Integrity

Passion

Priority-setting abilities

Team building skills

Trust

Vision

Vitality

How would you grade yourself in these areas?

All true leaders have different combinations of these skills, and varying styles, but the most effective leaders have superb people skills. They mingle with the general population, are easily approached and never lose sight of their company's mission. Paramount among their skills is the willingness to listen. The good Lord gave us two ears and one mouth. Good leaders listen twice as much as they speak.

Every Leader is Unique

Smart leaders have a secret: they know that people thrive most in an atmosphere of acceptance. When we have the permission to be authentic and unique, we are more contented and more productive. So aware leaders not only allow that uniqueness to blossom in the workplace, they express their own uniqueness—in style and personality. They show their human sides, talk with candor and display individual senses of humor. This helps erase the hierarchical gap that too often stifles enthusiasm in the workplace. When a leader holds firm to the mandate of the vision, and at the same time is approachable, the atmosphere becomes most conducive to results.

A final word about leaders, *passion* is contagious. When the man or woman at the top is honest and can be counted on, and at the same time is truly passionate about what he/she is doing, this passion surges through the company. Passionate people are easy to follow and they present the absolute best role models. The word enthusiasm means "god within". When a leader is enthusiastic, the energy in the arena rises.

It must be said here, that when I talk about leadership qualities, I include all strata of leadership. In one way or another, everybody in the organization, regardless of size, is a leader. We're all leading somebody.

The eight qualities listed below are essential for getting the job done efficiently and with the least amount of drag on the system. Any leader — meaning anyone who wants to blossom in their chosen calling—can gain great advantage mastering these qualities.

Leadership Qualities...including the ability to:

√ Build lasting teams

√ Encourage leadership skills in others

√ Create lasting impact with our companies and in our communities

√ Take risks and think outside the box

√ Create trust and foster loyalty

√ Take advantage of opportunities when presented, create opportunities when not

√ Recognize the potential in others

√ Have more fun

"The bible says 'A people without a vision shall perish.' Because you really can't deal with 'what is,' if you don't see that something better is about to come. Now, I can put up with losing my hair; I don't even mind losing a few teeth or getting a corn on my toe or a bunion on my foot (or something like that). But I got to have my eyes—because I got to be able to see what blessings are ahead of me."
—Bishop T.D. Jakes

Now, to help you understand your leadership competencies, complete the following exercise and then read on.

CHAPTER EIGHT EXERCISE

Reflect and respond to these questions:

1. Consider the eleven competencies discussed in this chapter when responding to each of the following questions. The eleven competencies are: *Courage, Creativity, Enthusiasm, Humor, Integrity, Passion, Priority-setting abilities, Team building skills, Trust, Vision, Vitality*

a. Which do you regard as most important for the work you do?

b. Which do you feel represents one of your strengths?

c. Which do you feel you need to work on the most?

d. How can you improve the competency(ies) which you have identified as needing the most work?

2. What can you do differently tomorrow as a result of reading this chapter?

3. Think for a minute about your own defining moments as a leader. Can you use any of these moments as stories that will aid the development of others?

LIFE-ESSENTIAL  9

No Individual Is an Island

Influencing the World around You

*"Success has nothing to do with what you gain in life or
accomplish for yourself. It's what you do for others."*
   —Danny Thomas

I n my opinion, we are living in the most interesting time in
the history of humankind. In the last century, we have
made more advancement—of every kind—than any other
era ever. We've taken huge strides in the fields of medicine,
computer science, communication technology and space explo-
ration. Today we take for granted everything from cellular
telephones with Internet access to the International Space
Station. Arguably, the greatest advancements have been in the
area of mass communication. With the push of a button, we can
communicate with just about anyone anywhere in the world
with the same clarity as if they were in the next room. And, if we
use email, we can even do this for little or no money. We can
ship any size parcel package anywhere on the planet and expect
it to get there within twenty-four hours.

The world may be the same physical size as it was a
hundred years ago, but it certainly seems a bit smaller today.
Modern innovation has produced powerful tools that continue

to bring everyone in the world closer and closer to one another. This fact opens up opportunities for greater, long-lasting international influence—politically, culturally, economically and otherwise.

The Most Influential Person of the Last 1000 Years

Who was the most influential person of the last thousand years? Was it Mother Teresa, Martin Luther King, Jr., Harriet Tubman, Mahatma Gandhi, Michelangelo, Abraham Lincoln, Albert Einstein, Princess Diana, Sir Isaac Newton, William Shakespeare, Thomas Jefferson, Adolf Hitler, Pablo Picasso, Nelson Mandela, Steven Spielberg, Florence Nightingale or Louie Armstrong? What about Bill Gates, Henry Ford, Thomas Edison, or Orville and Wilbur Wright?

While all of these people were certainly influential in the lives of millions, there is still one individual who was much more influential. The A&E television network posed this question to 360 journalists, scholars, and political leaders. Who do you think won?

The winner is... German inventor Johannes Gutenberg (1400-1468). He has influenced more lives in the last millennium than anyone dead or alive! Gutenberg developed the first method of utilizing movable type so that masses of written material could be printed with high speed and accuracy. Imagine not having your Sunday newspaper to relax with, imagine no textbooks in school, no transcripts in court, no yellow pages, no dictionary or thesaurus. What if every novel had to be hand-typed to be sold! Education, religion, business, politics, medicine—literally every field of study has enjoyed success because of the printed materials mass-produced by the brilliant invention of Gutenberg.

It seems rather certain that had Alexander Graham Bell never lived, the telephone would still have been invented around the same time in history. However, without Johannes Gutenberg, the invention of modern printing might have been delayed for many generations. His invention—shaping the course of Western civilization—remained the source of basic typesetting elements for over 500 years.

Hey, come to think of it, you wouldn't have this book in your hands if it weren't for Mr. Gutenberg. Thank you Johannes.

Tobacco & the Power of Influence

When the European settlers first encountered tobacco in America, little did they know what immense influence this mysterious plant would exert on the world! These late-15th-century settlers could hardly suspect the wealth—or the human misery—that tobacco would generate in future years. In fact, it has been reported that when Columbus arrived, the Natives gave Columbus gifts of fruit, wooden spears, and dried tobacco leaves. Columbus is said to have kept the other gifts but tossed the tobacco away! (Maybe he knew something the others didn't.)

At first, the early European settlers perceived the tobacco smoke produced by Native Americans as evidence of not only their supposed savagery, but also the plant's evil nature. But it didn't take long for the settlers to develop a taste for tobacco, and so it was eventually brought back to Europe to be cultivated and shared as one of the "treasures" of the New World.

Some Europeans were initially fearful and suspicious of tobacco, but later it was believed to have some positive medicinal effects—such as calming the nerves, curing headaches, and suppressing hunger. With time, recreational tobacco use became immensely popular. Aristocrats indulged their affinity for tobacco through ostentatious displays of snuff taken in fancy parlors. The working class and rebellious youth smoked tobacco in the streets and coffeehouses.

By the 1700s, the Royal Tobacco Factory at Seville had become Spain's largest employer and even the Vatican had its own tobacco factory. Later that century in America, Ben Franklin would use Virginian tobacco as collateral to finance the arming of Americans for the Revolutionary War!

Fast-forward two centuries: we find that tobacco has influenced the world to an amazing degree. For instance, in their last broad survey of U.S. tobacco use in 2000, the Center for Disease Control and Prevention (CDC) in Atlanta found that almost one in every four Americans (23.3 percent) smokes tobacco. In fact, the CDC considers tobacco use to be *the leading preventable cause of death* in the United States today! And while unknown to the Native Americans and European settlers, much has been learned over the last forty years about the negative effects of tobacco on our health. There is clear evidence that tobacco use causes chronic lung and heart disease, as well as cancer of the lungs, esophagus, mouth and bladder. Accumulating research regarding tobacco's dark side have been a factor in America's decreasing smoking rates. About fifty years ago, approximately 75 percent of American men smoked!

Unfortunately, tobacco smoking is on the increase in other parts of the world, as barriers to trade markets fall. Overall, according to the World Bank, one in three people on Earth smoke today. In South Korea, which has the highest rates for both its adult and youth populations, seventy percent of men smoke. Roughly sixty percent of males in China and Japan smoke, and men smoke at this same rate in Eastern and Central Europe. In Latin America, forty percent of men smoke. (Note: Women smoke at lower rates in all of these regions.) Sadly, three million people around the world are now dying every year from tobacco-related causes!

Even while tobacco is inflicting a huge cost on our American society, as well as the global community at large, in terms of both quality of life and shortened life span, promotion of tobacco products has certainly not stopped. Obviously generators of messages promoting tobacco use do not have our best interests in mind! For them, there is much at stake. In the U.S. alone, where the gross domestic national product approaches $8 trillion, tobacco products and services account for almost seven percent!

Obviously the story of tobacco is truly a story about the power of influence. Some might say that tobacco has "come a long way, baby," since those first European settlers watched Native Americans smoke tobacco in their ceremonies. Still it seems like the right time to turn the influence around. Help someone quit smoking today! Tobacco kills! Interestingly, cessation programs have begun in Native American communities, where cigarette use now is more prevalent than ceremonial tobacco use. Native Americans have some of the highest rates for cigarette smoking found in the U.S. today—almost 33.5 percent. According to the CDC, lung cancer is currently the leading cause of cancer death among Native Americans.

"People who treat other people as less than human must not be surprised when the bread they have cast on the waters comes back to them, poisoned."

—James Baldwin

Don't Stop at Thirty-Two

When Cathy Hughes was a young girl growing up in the housing projects of Omaha, Nebraska, she knew that someday she would have a career in radio. Her mother gave her a radio when Cathy was eight years old, and she listened to it incessantly. She stayed up late at night listening to her favorite programs. Her very favorite was the outrageous Wolfman Jack, arguably the leading voice in rock 'n' roll radio in the 60s.

Cathy attended Creighton University and the University of Nebraska at Omaha but did not graduate. The pull from radio was too strong. In 1969 she began working at KOWH, a black radio station in Omaha. She handled various jobs and did well enough that she was offered a job as lecturer at the School of Communications at Howard University in Washington, DC. In 1973, she became sales director at the university's radio station WHUR. Two years later she became the first female vice president and general manager of a station in the nation's capital. Sales revenue went from $300,000 to $3.5 million in one year.

Cathy was a whiz at increasing revenue, but what she really loved was programming. She wanted the radio to inspire people's souls. In the same year she was promoted to general manager, she created the *Quiet Storm*—which would become the most listened to nighttime radio format, heard in over 50 markets nationally. The *Quiet Storm* was aimed toward the female listener, a blend of love songs, tunes that would uplift the spirit and make the audience feel warm and fuzzy all over. Cathy Hughes' *Quiet Storm* is still a great favorite in the urban market.

Cathy was only getting started. Subsequently, she created another great success. She saw a need and filled it —always the sign of a great entrepreneur! Cathy realized that black people in particular loved to listen to gospel music, but that they could often only listen at night. So she created the 24-hour gospel station. About the same time, the shareholders of the station demanded that Cathy focus more on generating income. Cathy balked. One of the stockholders said something like, "Then why don't you just leave and start your own radio station?"

As so often occurs, happenstance helped direct Cathy's destiny. She decided to do just that, and armed with a thorough business plan, and a strong dose of self-confidence, she waded through *thirty-two rejections* from male bankers until a female banker took a chance on her. In 1979, she and her husband, Dewey Hughes, purchased a small Washington radio station, WOL, creating Radio One. In time, Cathy's marriage ended and she bought Dewey's share in the station. For a time, money was so tight that she had to give up her apartment and live at the station. Eventually, the station created a profit, and her own talk show became a hit.

Spurred by success, Cathy purchased other stations. Today Radio One is the nations largest black-owned radio chain and the first African American company in radio history to dominate several major markets simultaneously. Cathy Hughes has been a true pathfinder, creating a number of precedents. Among them, Cathy is the first African American woman to head a publicly traded firm on a stock exchange in the United States.

Cathy Hughes could have let her dream die back in the late 70s. Most of us would have just given up long before the thirty-second rejection. Instead, these rejections spurred Cathy Hughes on. She never lost sight of her dream. She knew she had a strong vision, and a well-researched business plan, so she just kept moving towards her goal.

Today, Cathy Hughes' radio stations reach over eighteen million black listeners daily. Radio One, Inc. currently employs more than 1,500 black broadcasters in more than fifty stations nationwide. Because Cathy didn't give up, she has been able to share on an ever-widening scale her great support for under-represented communities, her indomitable entrepreneurial spirit and her dedication to the empowerment of women.

"It's not over 'til you win!"
—Les Brown

Mass Media and You

Television, radio, film, the Internet, and magazines are such persuasive mediums because they can magically make things appear real when, in fact, they may not be. Of all these mediums, television has the greatest influence. It has the ability to project visual images, matched with a musical theme, song, or jingle, sending an emotional message with either a positive or negative spin.

TELEVISION = TELL A VISION

See the slogan above? Doesn't TV do just that?—it tells us about a vision that is almost always not our own. Often others design this vision mainly for their benefit. This is particularly true of commercials that tell the vision of the benefits offered by a particular product. Television has so (1) *overexposed* our culture to negative imagery that we have (2) become *de-sensitized* to these negative images, and we nonchalantly (3) *rationalize* away the same things that once upon a time were so offensive.

Overexposure: Twenty years ago, children were rarely exposed to the vulgarity that heavily saturates present-day television programming. Today we have trashy talk shows like those hosted by Jerry Springer; Jerry's guests constantly curse, discuss their sex scandals and expose their bodies. Many music videos exploit women's sexuality in order to sell records. To keep us hooked, the evening news parades dangerous police chases, shoot-outs, bloody murders, madness and mindless mayhem.

On television, everyone gets in the act. Commercials for restaurant chains promote the negative value that *bigger is always better* by offering super-sized meal deals, knowing that this food contributes to obesity and deteriorating health. This kind of advertising helps create the need for super-sized bath towels to cover super-sized rear ends.

De-sensitized: The end result of desensitization is that our society thinks the influence of negative exposure is no big deal anymore. It seems that we've become immune to foul language and partial nudity on network TV, as well as the uncensored cursing that punctuates several popular radio programs. Thirty years ago, Victoria Secret models in nothing but thong underwear would not have been allowed in public. Today, it's no big deal. In addition, it's commonplace on TV to feature abuse against women by men, and research shows that such images can influence men to think such behavior is okay. I once saw a domestic violence poster in a hospital which said this about a battered woman: he beat her 150 times—the only time he gave her flowers was at her funeral. At this rate, what will be the norm for violence and vulgarity in our media thirty years from now?

Rationalizing: Each year it seems the overall content of television programming becomes even riskier. TV networks appear to care far less about morality or social responsibility than they do their ratings (the bottom line that produces vast earnings for their respective companies). The media status quo takes another dip and we rationalize it away. We see so much degradation and low life that it no longer shocks us. We develop an attitude of that's just the way it is. As Spike Lee once said, "We should try our best to do the right thing, and while we're at it—do that thing right!"

"I wish there was a knob on the TV to turn up the INTELLIGENCE. There's a knob called 'brightness', but it doesn't work!"
—Gallagher

That's Why They Call it Programming

"Mirror, mirror on the screen, what's the point of what we've seen?"
—Anonymous

I am greatly affected by a comparison I heard somewhere regarding the influences on our youth in the 1950s versus today. The comparison makes profound sense, but I hadn't considered it this way, and it truly shook me up. Especially when we look at the incredible challenges facing our young people today.

The chart below prioritizes the factors influencing youth today as compared with fifty years ago.

1950s	**Today**
1. Family	1. Media
2. Religion	2. Peers
3. School	3. School
4. Peers	4. Religion
5. Media	5. Family

CONSIDER THIS:

1950s...

In the 1950s most families didn't own a TV set. Likely there was a radio or two, but there was really no such thing as the mass media. Young people got the news from the newspaper or from friends and family members.

Today...

98% of American homes have televisions (more than those that have indoor plumbing).

50% of homes with children aged two to seventeen have at least one TV, a VCR, video game equipment, and a home computer.

Three out of every five children ages twelve to seventeen have televisions in their own rooms.

The typical American family keeps the TV on 7.5 to 9 hours every day.

In addition to television, time is spent watching movies, listening to music (which some studies show to be more than forty hours per week), watching videos, playing video or computer games, or surfing the Internet.

1950s...

Sex, drugs, alcohol, crime and violence were not glamorized on TV, in the movies or in the print media. Sex, violence and mayhem were not yet *cool*.

Today...

The average kid is exposed to more than 13,000 sexual references each year.

80% of the movies produced annually are unsuitable for kids under age thirteen.

The typical teenager sees fifty R-rated movies or videos each year—nearly one per week.

The average child watches up to 8,000 made-for-TV murders and 100,000 acts of violence by the end of grade school. By the age of sixteen, the typical child has witnessed an estimated 200,000 acts of violence, including 33,000 murders.
(The American Psychological Association)

1950s...

Families had just about every meal together. Personal and social issues would be discussed. The kitchen table was a sacred place where good, wholesome food and conversation was shared.

Daddy worked, mama stayed home with the kids and took care of the house. One income was enough. Everyone was home at night. The family played games and acted like a family.

Kids had paper routes, mowed lawns and babysat. This way they earned some money on their own and learned a lesson or two about responsibility.

On Sunday, families went to church together.

Today… Kids today spend an average of 1500
hours per year watching television, less than
1000 hours in school, and *an average of 66 hours*
per year in conversation with their parents.
Mama spends about 35 minutes a day with her
children; daddy (if he's present in the household)
averages 7 minutes per day.

What can one conclude from all of this? First and foremost: the world of our young people has been turned totally
upside down. Today, in almost all of our households—when
there are two parents, and often there is only one—both mom
and dad have full-time jobs. We have become a consumerist
society—we want our things—and we've left the job of raising
our kids to street-life and the media. (Cut it any way you want,
whoever spends the most time with our children is doing the
raising.)

The consequence is obvious. Without responsible guidance that emphasizes wholesome values, our young people are
left with a distorted sense of right and wrong. Nowhere is this
more obvious than in our inner cities. When a stable, steadying
home life is missing, the pervasive influence of provocative
music lyrics, drug dealers and gangs predominate. Since dealing
drugs and breaking the law is made to look so *cool* in the media,
making $150,000 or more a year selling drugs looks likes a
winner when compared with earning $45,000 per year upon
college graduation.

There's only one way to combat these statistics: put the
family back on top. It's doubtful that the media is going to
govern itself into a more balanced state of affairs, but if we give
the job of raising our kids back to mama and papa, we stand a
chance of putting things in perspective.

After all, as long as our society continues to allow them
to—we can't really complain when we see how effectively the
media has seduced our children and shaped their beliefs and
points of view. That's why they call it programming.

"We forfeit three-quarters of ourselves in order to be like other people."

—Arthur Schopenhauer

Scared Straight at Nellis

Remember the award-winning documentary *Scared Straight?* I was nine-years-old when I first saw it. The film is a great example of how we can change people's thinking and thereby improve their behaviors by using the resources of the media. *Scared Straight* documented a program in which juveniles with destructive or delinquent behaviors were brought to prison where inmate volunteers helped to change the youngsters' mindsets—especially regarding imprisonment.

At the beginning of the program, these kids were tough and hardheaded. They said that going to prison would not bother them a bit. In fact, some thought it would be cool to go, since they had friends and relatives who had been to jail. However, after being locked up for a short period with hardened criminals serving time for assault and battery, murder, rape, and armed robbery, their viewpoints shifted—almost instantly. Those teenagers had been scared for their lives!

Dr. James T. Martinoff, my finance professor at Pepperdine University, created a similar program just for MBAs. It's better known as *Scared Straight: The Club Fed Edition.* Just as in the original 1978 documentary, the program at Pepperdine aims to produce high regard for ethics and integrity. Dr. Martinoff took us MBA candidates to Nellis Air Force Base, which houses the federal prison camp in hot Las Vegas, Nevada.

At Nellis, the other MBA candidates and I met with white-collar prisoners *who were a lot like us—they had similar drives and ambitions, but obviously went a little too far.* The prisoners had exchanged their power neckties for khaki uniforms, and six and seven-figure salaries to earn a measly twelve pennies an hour doing boring tasks at the adjacent Air Force Base. I must say that my experience during my visit at Nellis was mind-blowing. One of the panelists told us: *"don't be naïve about innocent people being sent to prison. The prison industry is geared to having a constant flow of cattle."* In other words, the prison industry will never be under-populated.

In a survey conducted by Dr. Martinoff, half of his students said that they had made unethical business decisions in the past, and more than one-third realized that some of their prior business transactions might have been criminal. Nearly ninety percent of his alumni reported that the Scared Straight program for MBAs gave them an ethical anchor for making future business decisions.

"If you want to know your past – look into your present conditions.
If you want to know your future – look into your present actions!"
—Chinese Proverb

Effective Communication

Being a parent is one of the greatest privileges in my life. Personally, I believe the purpose of children is to help their parents learn more about themselves. At least that's the case with me. Everyday, I learn so much from my kids—especially in the way we communicate with each other. Of my three children, my middle child Ahsaan is the funniest. By the time Ahsaan was three years old, he had already said the darndest things. Many of them were based on misunderstandings due to his young age.

Honeymoon: In a hallway of our home, Ahsaan stared at a framed picture on the wall of my wife and me on our honeymoon. Aloria and I were kissing at one end of a Carnival cruise ship as the sun set on the Mexican Riviera. Ahsaan asked, *Dad, are you and Mommy at the beach?* I said, *No Son, we're on a cruise ship on our honeymoon.* Puzzled he said, *Honeymoon—Dad, what's that?* I replied, *You see, Son, when you finish pre-school, you're gonna go on to elementary school.* Ahsaan said, *Yeah Dad, elementary school!* Then I said, *Next you're gonna go to middle school and high school.* He said, *Yeah Dad, high school!* Then I said, *Son, after high school, you're gonna go to college, then graduate school!* Ahsaan said, *Yeah Dad, graduate schoooooool!* And I said, *Yeah Son, during graduate school you'll meet and date a beautiful young lady. And then the two of you will become engaged.* He said, *Yeah Dad, engaged!* And lastly, I said, *Then after your engagement—you two will marry.*

Ahsaan paused, and then said with pure excitement, *Yeah Dad, —Mary had a little lamb!* Boy, that made me laugh so hard—I never got to explain what a honeymoon was.

Going Fishing: One Saturday morning, Ahsaan and I were watching *Stanley*, a favorite cartoon of his on The Disney Channel. One of the characters was fishing on the show and Ahsaan said to me, *Ooh Dad, I want to go fishing. Will you take me fishing?* I replied, *Sure Son, I'll take you fishing!* He asked, *When Dad, when?* I said, *When you get a little older.* He said, *Okay Dad, then let's go tomorrow!*

Dinosaurs: My wife Aloria and my son Ahsaan were reading animal books together. One book was about dinosaurs, and my wife began explaining the history of this kind of animal. She told Ahsaan that they lived millions of years ago, but were now *extinct.* Ahsaan looked at his mom and said, *Yeah mommy, they smell like stinky boo boo.*

Pick Up That Flyer: Coming in the front door of our home, I noticed that a one-sheet advertisement had been slid under the door. My hands were full of grocery bags, so I asked Ahsaan to pick up the flyer for me. I looked back behind me and saw him looking all around the doorway. I said, *Ahsaan, pick up that flyer right there!* Confused he looked to his right, then over to his left, and then under his legs. He said, *Dad, where is it?* I said, *Ahsaan, pick up that flyer—right there next to your foot.* He said pointing his finger downward, *This?* I said, *Yes, that!* He said to me, *Dad, this is not a flyer—this is a piece of paper. It can't fly.* Well, what could I say—Ahsaan was only going by what he knew. That's my son.

Christmas: Each year on Christmas day, my wife's side of our family usually gathers to exchange hundreds of gifts and enjoy a big feast. On Ahsaan's third Christmas he was truly excited! He led our circle of family and friends in prayer as we blessed the food. After we finished the prayer, he made a special request that we sing "Happy Birthday" for Jesus. And so we did. When we were finished, Ahsaan shouted out, *Happy birthday Jesus! Now blow out the candles!*

In order to influence others in a positive way, we have to know how to communicate effectively. In business, poor communication can lead to disaster and financial ruin. In international affairs, it can lead to war. In personal relationships, poor communication can lead to partners becoming strangers and eventually drifting apart.

In order for a personal or professional relationship to be fulfilling, we must understand the other party's needs. There are different strokes for different folks.

This is certainly true for my wife Aloria and me. For example, when it comes to conversations, Aloria mostly enjoys them just for the sake of us talking to one another. I usually engage in the conversation as a means to an end.

No question about it, understanding the needs of those we desire to have a personal or professional relationship with is one of the most important keys in communicating effectively. I've learned that the more I *love* my wife, the more she *supports* me in my endeavors. My philosophy is this: *The more I water her flowers, the more beautiful they continue to grow—and she helps me to do my thing.*

Another important factor in communicating effectively goes back to something I mentioned earlier from that old proverb—*we are given one mouth and two ears.* This is so we can listen twice as much as we talk. You can't listen and talk at the same time. Keep your mouth closed and your ears open. Listen with your mind as well as your ears. If you're busy thinking about what you're going to say next, you're not listening. Keep your mind focused on what the other person is saying, then— *when it's your turn*—think five times before you speak. Lastly, listen with your heart. Watch for the nonverbal clues that tell you what the other person is really saying.

"You will have many opportunities in life to keep your mouth shut. You should take advantage of every one of them."
—Thomas Alva Edison

As Ye Sow, So Shall Ye Reap

In engineering school at Cal State Northridge, I studied The Three Laws of Sir Isaac Newton. Of his three laws of physics, it was the first law that made an indelible impression on my mind. Newton's first law also called *The Law of Inertia*, states that *a body at rest remains at rest and a body in motion continues to move at a constant velocity unless acted upon by an external force.* Another way of saying it is: *For every action, there is an equal and opposite reaction.*

This same law can be applied to our daily lives. The *accolades* we can expect in our lives will always be matched by the amount of service we provide to other people. Our primary purpose on earth is to serve others and to receive service from others. Picture, if you can, a huge balance scale, similar to the kind held in the hands of *"the blind gal, Lady Justice."* This type of scale has a cross arm over the fulcrum from which hang two large gold plates. One of the plates is marked *Compensation* and the other plate is labeled *Service*. Whatever we place onto the *Service* plate , society will match in the form of *Compensation*. How we conduct our lives—in the way we feel, the way we perform, the words we speak—this is what we place onto the gold plate labeled *Service*. The *amount* and the *spirit* of our service will decide our compensation.

The greatest way to influence the world around you is to provide world-class service. If you're dissatisfied with your rewards, think about the extent of your service to others. Remember what Sir Isaac Newton taught us: *For every action, there is an equal and opposite reaction.* "No deposit, no return" is the policy. Only what a person puts out into this world can he expect in return. This is called reciprocity; we reap exactly what we sow, all the days of our lives.

Brand Yourself

When you think *Volvo*, you might think of *safety*. When you think *Home Depot*, you might think *Do It Yourself*. When you think *Nike*, you might think *Tiger Woods* or *LeBron James* or *Just Do It*. When people need to wrap a sandwich, they ask for *Saran Wrap*. We often refer to ordinary powder bathroom cleansers as

Comet or *Ajax*. People usually ask for *Vaseline*, not petroleum jelly—regardless of the actual name printed on the label. It doesn't matter who really made it, many people refer to all cola sodas as *Coke*. That's because, for many of us, *Coke* is synonymous for all colas in general. Why is this? The answer is *branding*. These examples demonstrate the powerful influence that major product brands have on the minds of everyday people.

One might ask the question, "What exactly is a brand?" *Is it a trademark or logo design? Is it a slogan or a jingle? Is it that thing that ranchers burn into the hides of cattle?* Actually, the word "brand" came to us from that thing they burn into cattle; a rancher sears the hide of his cattle with a distinctive mark so that his animals won't be confused with anyone else's. His brand is his identity.

In modern usage, brand identity consists of brand names, logos, positioning, brand associations, and brand personality. An effective brand name gives a good first impression and evokes positive associations. A brand personifies what business a company is in, what benefits it gives, and why it is better than the competition. The same is true for an individual person. What is your brand or reputation? What do other people think of you? What talent or value do they associate with your name?

As is true with business brands, how others perceive you is strongly influenced by their first impression of you. However, repetitive impressions also count.

Derek Lee Armstrong and Kam Wai Yu, co-authors of *The Persona Principle: How to Succeed in Business with Image Marketing,* propose that the system of creating a marketable image or life brand for yourself is based on these truths:

- Your image is power.

- Be perceived as the best and you will become your best.

- Your reputation is more important than your bank account.

• There is more value in appearing successful than in being successful.

The Persona Principle™ states that *image is more valuable than resources or skills to any aspiring entrepreneur, salesperson, manager, or corporate officer.*

In his groundbreaking book *Build Your Own Life Brand*, best-selling author and business consultant Stedman Graham suggests that we should use branding—the technique employed by major advertisers to distinguish their products—for our own benefit. He says: *"Think for a minute about the people you value most in your work, your relationships, and the organizations or groups you belong to. They have skills, knowledge, or personal characteristics that add to the quality of your life. Their "brands" or reputations carry a promise. The individuals who stand out in the world around us are those who offer the greatest value to the most people—just as those products with the strongest brands are the ones that offer us the greatest value."*

Whether you realize it or not, you are already pitching your own "brand" every day in many different ways—perhaps as an undergraduate college student hoping to make the grades for graduate school, as an actor competing for a role in a new movie, or as a entrepreneur striving to stay two steps ahead of the competition.

Why is branding important for you? It's a method of creating a distinct identity that will make you stand out from the crowd. That way, people will know your strengths, and you will be in a better position to be a positive influence in your world.

"You'd make an awful someone else, but you would make a wonderful you!"
—Anonymous

Life-Essential Nine Exercise

1. Now that you've learned that your rewards in life must be in clear-cut proportion to your service, how will you increase the quality of your service today?

2. What talents, information, skills, and personal uniqueness do you have that add value to the lives of those around you?

3. What significant value do you attach to:

   • Your business or employer?

   • Your circle of family and friends?

   • Your co-workers, classmates, associations, organizations, neighbors, etc.?

4. What can you do to develop your strengths so that you stand out from other people in your line of work, in your relationships, and in your other circles?

5. What personal contributions or strengths do you consider most important:

   • In your work?

   • In your relationships?

   • In your community life?

   • In your family life?

6. What is your most distinguishing characteristic —the way others differentiate you? Think about your employer and colleagues, family members, close friends, neighbors, and acquaintances.

LIVING WHILE MAKING A LIVING

Creating Balance

*"We cannot be happy if we expect to live all the time at the highest
peal of intensity. Happiness is not a matter of intensity, but of
balance and order and rhythm and harmony."*
—Thomas Merton

While you need to master the life-skills for staying
on track with your daily activities, it's vital to
realize that making a living is a means to an end.
This chapter should kick-start your thinking
about creating a style of living that results in balance and a sense
of overall well-being. Your life should support who you are and
where you are in every area. This approach will help you feel
good about yourself and achieve the fulfillment and great life
everyone desires.

*"If I had my life to live over, I would start barefoot earlier in the
spring and stay that way later in the fall."*
—Nadine Stair (at eighty-five years of age)

Is It Rocking Chair Material?

Is it important enough for another gray hair?
Do I need to sweat it, do I need to swear?
Is it bad enough to be sheddin' tears?
Is it big enough that in fifty years...
I'll be talking 'bout it in my rockin' chair?

We're living in a hyper-active age. There is always too much to do, and seemingly, too little time to do it. Our ancestors devoted most of their waking moments to making sure they had food to eat. We have thousands of choices of food-services primed and ready to provide us as much food as we want—as fast we want it. It's strange, if you think about it, every day there is a new advancement of some kind that makes everything easier and faster. Yet, the end result is more choices and seemingly less time. Balance is life's little conundrum.

Stress and worry is the enemy of balance. The more energy I put into fretting about my life, grousing about the past, worrying about the future, ruing my decisions—the harder it is to maintain a semblance of balance.

Does it matter this much, do I really care?
Is it all so crucial, is it so unfair?
Is it so darned tricky that I can't shift gears?
Is it big enough that in fifty years...
I'll be talking 'bout it in my rockin' chair?

Fortunately, I have a code I apply to everything. I call it: *Is it Rocking Chair Material?* When I'm stressing over one of those life situations that can consume all your energy if you let it—an argument with my wife, a failed business decision, a traffic ticket—I ask myself: *"Is it Rocking Chair Material?"* In other words, will it matter when I'm eighty? When I'm old and gray—and I do plan on getting old and gray in the (very) distant future—is this situation today important enough that I will be reminiscing about it with my fellow rocker(s)?

Thankfully, most of the things that pop up on a day-to-day basis are not life-changing or life-threatening, and consequently not good rocking chair material. Just knowing that keeps things in the *molehill* category.

Frankly, the biggest secret I have about balance springs from this rocking chair concept: it is a whole lot easier to maintain balance in our lives when we *release all unnecessary drama*. After all, what we're balancing in the first place is the *be* versus the *do*. When the *do* carries with it a lot of superfluous histrionics, the *be* can get overwhelmed.

> *Am I really that lost in deep despair?*
> *Am I really so dense and unaware?*
> *Is it really that hard to face my fears?*
> *Is it big enough that in fifty years...*
> *I'll be talking 'bout it in my rockin' chair?*

The next time a situation pops up that seems oh-so-important and wants to ruin your day/week/month/life, ask yourself this simple question: "Is it Rocking Chair Material?"

"Stop acting as if life is a rehearsal. Live this day as if it were your last. The past is over and gone. The future is not guaranteed."
—Dr. Wayne W. Dyer

From Career Triumph to Family Tragedy

One day on a radio call-in show, I heard a man talk about how a job opportunity that he was offered turned into a family disaster. I'll refer to the man as Roger. Though I don't remember the real names of all the people that were involved, this man's story has stayed with me for years.

Roger's boss Henry called him into the office one day. After praising Roger for his leadership on a project, Henry said that the company had decided that Roger was the best person to become "head honcho" of a newly created division of the company. The new job would start in one month. It would require that Roger and his family move from the quiet Southern town that was home to the company's headquarters to a city in the Midwest.

Roger was thrilled. He felt the opportunity was perfect for him. He knew that many of his peers at the large international company would envy this career move. The next day, after talking it over with his somewhat-reluctant wife Sherry, Roger accepted the offer. The family moved to the midwestern city right on schedule. Excelling in the new executive position, Roger adapted to it easily, though the job demanded a lot of overtime.

The family had been living at the new location for about six months when Sherry asked Roger to drive their fourteen-year-old daughter Carey to school because of a scheduling conflict with a doctor's appointment. During the drive, Carey complained that she had no friends at the new school even though she had been popular in her hometown. Roger made light of it, thinking this was just part of the transition. He told his daughter to give it a little more time. Though Carey tried to talk to her dad about this issue again at different times, he never took the problem to heart.

It wasn't until the next school year that Carey really clicked with one of her classmates—Dana. The two girls seemed inseparable. But then the phone call came from a school administrator. It seemed that Carey had developed a crack habit and Dana was a big influence in this. The two girls appeared to be skipping school to do the drug.

It was Sherry who took the call from the school. She immediately called her husband at work, even though he didn't like to be disturbed on the job. Though shaken by the news, Roger tried to appear calm and reassured his wife that he would handle it at home that night.

Roger was never really able to handle it. The more he tried to control his daughter, the wilder she became. When Carey was grounded, she always found a way to sneak out. Making sure she stayed in school during the day seemed impossible. Screaming arguments between father and daughter developed into a regular part of the family scene. In fact, the family's entire home-life was going downhill. The middle daughter, Kathy, who had been a model student, had trouble sleeping and began to bring home slipping grades. And their youngest child, eight-year-old Jimmy, started getting into arguments with his classmates.

Finally, Roger had enough. He called the police and Carey was put in jail for drug possession. Roger thought this would teach her a lesson. Instead, when she was released, Carey got her younger sister Kathy involved with crack too. Now the two girls would both argue with Dad.

Finally, there was a knock on the front door in the middle of the night. Roger opened the door and saw two police officers. One officer asked, *"Do you have a daughter named Carey?"* *"Yes,"* Roger answered. *"Do you know where she is right now?"* Roger said that he hoped Carey was in the house but that she sometimes sneaked out. The first officer responded, *"Sir, there's been a report that your daughter Carey, a girl named Dana, and a young man just committed a grand theft of an automobile. They are traveling out of state. Your daughter is still at large and is being chased by state troopers..."*

During the radio show, Roger said that, at that moment, he wished he had the power to turn back the hands of time. Roger admitted that all he had been thinking about when told about the job promotion was his own career. This father never considered how the move might affect his children. He had taken his stable home-life for granted. Roger never imagined that the police would be knocking on his front door because his daughter Carey stole an automobile!

Roger's story is a cautionary tale. Part of achieving balance is remembering to take care of those loved ones who take care of us and to also care for the other family members who need our attention!

"The most meaningful job of a successful Dad is to create wonderful memories for his whole family."
—Tony Magee, MS, MBA

Balancing Act

Especially in this day and age, life is like walking a tightrope. If you put too much weight in your career you fall over to the right side. If you focus so much on your personal life—health, family and friends—that you don't take care of business, you tumble to the left. Having said that, there is a net on your left flank. If you over-emphasize your well-being, your family and your loved ones, you bounce in the net and can just dust yourself off and get back on the rope. But if you over-emphasize work to the detriment of intimate relationships, the fall is inglorious. The damage to health, and to those you hold close can be irreparable. Additionally, stress and burnout can result from a life out-of-balance.

The key to staying in balance is to name and claim those things that bring you fulfillment. If you put your focus on these items, you will stay in balance and be able to journey across the rope with relative ease. Here's a partial list of these items. Put a checkmark next to the categories that bring you happiness and satisfaction— yet are too often missing in your life.

☐ Connection with others
☐ Entertainment
☐ Exercise
☐ Giving and Sharing
☐ Humor
☐ Play
☐ Routine
☐ Solitude and Stillness
☐ Spirituality
☐ Travel
☐ Variety

Next, ask yourself how you can make time for the things that you marked. These are the keys to balancing your life. The task to balance one's life can be daunting. Look around. There are not a lot of people living genuinely balanced lives. It's not easy, but it's definitely attainable. As you begin to re-prioritize, remember the following: 1) be genuine and authentic; 2) be as present as possible; 3) nurture yourself; 4) reach out to others.

"If you want happiness for an hour – take a nap. If you want happiness for a day—go fishing. If you want happiness for a month—get married. If you want happiness for a year—inherit a fortune. If you want happiness for a lifetime—help someone else."

—Chinese Proverb

If You Work Hard, You Should Play Hard

If you work hard, you should play hard. You've got to have some fun. When people don't realize this, they burn out. They also become frustrated. No matter what it is that you love to do, eventually you need to pull away and replenish yourself. Otherwise, you'll become depleted; this is what causes highly successful people to become alcoholics and drug addicts, to suffer depression, to consider suicide. The harder the work, then the harder the recreation should be. These elements should be in direct proportion to each other. Don't skip that vacation!

"Once a year, go someplace you've never been before."

—The Dalai Lama

"Finish each day and be done with it. You have done what you could. Some blunders and absurdities no doubt crept in; forget them as soon as you can. Tomorrow is a new day; begin it well and serenely and with too high a spirit to be cumbered with your old nonsense."

—Ralph Waldo Emerson

24 Hours—That's It!

Have you ever let a disappointment get you down for days on end? Well, there's a technique available that can help you process just about any type of intense emotion— elation, anger, pride, fear, etc.— without getting stuck in it.

The method is called the *"24-Hour Rule."* The idea is that you allow yourself to fully feel the emotion for a total of twenty-four hours—and that's it! Once twenty-four hours have passed, you move on to the next thing life has set before you.

The 24-Hour Rule was created by Don Schula, the former head coach of the Miami Dolphin football team. He used it and insisted that his players and coaches did too. Schula didn't want to see them gloating over a win or moping over a loss for more than a day. Ken Blanchard also endorses this technique in his book, *The Heart of a Leader*.

Try the Rule out! It works. The coach and Ken Blanchard are right! In the long run, you'll feel better for allowing the feelings to surface rather than pushing them down. And you'll see that what matters is not the daily victories and defeats, it's being the best person you can be in all circumstances.

"Yesterday is a cancelled check. Tomorrow is a promissory note. Today is the only cash you have. So spend it wisely."
  —Anonymous

"Set aside half an hour every day to do all your worrying, then take a nap during this period."
  —Anonymous

If You Don't Know, You Better Ask Somebody

"You create your opportunities by asking for them."
  —Patty Hansen

Another important aspect of creating a well-balanced life is asking for what it is that you want—for what your heart desires. In their best-selling book *The Aladdin Factor*, Jack Canfield and Mark Victor Hansen emphasized this major point exactly. Read their book to learn even more about the process of asking.

Asking for help can be one of the toughest things for us to do. For some odd reason, many of us prefer to do things the hard way. For instance, we walk into a department store, and rather than look at the directory or ask questions, we wander around looking for things.

Now, we all know that it saves time and effort to get the straight scoop right away. Are we trying to "prove ourselves" —to demonstrate that we're of higher intellect and instinctively keen? *I don't need anybody showing me the way to go! I can find it on my own!*

This particular quirk rears its ugly head in many situations in life. Of course, driving a car without asking for directions heads the list for many men, so we waste hours of our lives not knowing exactly how to get where we're going.

It's normal to feel like we need to do everything ourselves; the American society places a high value on the unrealistic goal of doing it all alone. This attitude shows up in such behavior as perfectionism, which has reached the level of a disease in our culture. Perfectionists believe that not only should they do it all themselves, but they should also do it perfectly with a smile on their faces!

This ideal is nothing but a fantasy, of course. We all feel the crush of conflicting demands on our time, energy, and psyche. We also feel anger and resentment when pushed beyond our limits. After all, we're not going to do our best when we're tired and frustrated.

Asking for help is not a sign of weakness or failure; it's an act of wisdom. We are empowering ourselves. Bringing a different perspective and another set of skills and expertise in to solve a problem may be exactly what's needed. Also, when we ask for help, we're often empowering the person we're asking. We're saying that we see them as competent and knowledgeable. That's our gift to them in return for their effort.

Here are seven points to consider when you're in need of assistance:

1. *Remember, it's a good thing to ask for help. Don't be embarrassed, and don't worry about what others have to say about it.*

2. *Getting help when you need it is part of being responsible —to yourself and to your team.*

3. *Think what might happen if you don't get help—or if you do!*

4. Decide what the problem is and what help you need.

5. Think about whom you could ask for help. Choose someone you trust, who you know has the knowledge to help you—not just any ol' body!

6. Think about what you'll say when you ask for help.

7. Then, just do it!

"You don't always get what you ask for, but you never get what you don't ask for... unless it's contagious!"
　　　　—Franklyn Broude

"And I say unto you, ask, and it shall be given you; seek, and ye shall find; knock, and it shall be opened unto you. For everyone that asketh receiveth; and he that seeketh findeth; And to him that knocketh it shall be opened."
　　　　—Luke 11:9 and 10

Want to Know How to Live?
Forgive...Forgive...Forgive!

"Why do we allow someone who's nasty to us rent so much space in our minds."
　　　　—Frederic Luskin

In Webster's, the definition for the word forgive is *to give up resentment or a claim for requital,* but I don't think the definition goes far enough. I think it should include something like *and a divine act that guarantees better physical and mental health for the forgiving party and a full reprieve for the party forgiven.* Holding grudges is a flat-out certainty that the grudge-holder will suffer —in many cases much more than the other party. Research shows that when people were asked to focus on someone who wronged them, their moods darkened, their heart rates and blood pressure rose. This did not happen for those who were thinking about forgiveness.

Forgiveness is a brand-new day after a heavy rain. The air is fresh, the atmosphere is clean, life is renewed.

There have been a number of studies on forgiveness, the most impressive—at least to me—done by Frederic Luskin and Diana Robinson, PhD. at Stanford University. They asked three questions regarding forgiveness: *What is it? Why forgive? What are the steps to forgiveness?*

The results of the study were interesting. Most people didn't even know what forgiveness was. (If you were thinking the same thing, see...you're not alone.) Whatever definition you want to choose, forgiveness is an act of compassion. It's a positive action. Forgiveness is not about going into denial. (*"What are you talking about? I don't really remember."*) And it's not about sweeping the grievance under the rug. (*"Oh, no problem, it was nothing."*)

Here's the thing, if you don't forgive, you continue to replicate the schism. Bitterness dominates. Both parties suffer. Usually, the "grieved" party suffers the most, dredging up the past over and over again. Your natural flow stops, you become a robot to satisfy the pain and injustice. Self-esteem tumbles, your values slip off the chart and into the middle of the pity party.

Granted, in some sectors of our culture, non-forgiveness is a way of life. Look at the situation in the Holy Land. Without true forgiveness, an eye-for-an-eye consciousness dominates. Some of our families are the same way. False pride eliminates the possibility of forgiveness. Family members and one-time friends can be cast out of the heart, never to return. What a waste! What an insult to health and well-being. Even if that's your heritage, forgiveness is learnable.

Here's a stab at the steps it takes to create forgiveness in your life. Remember these things:

It's not really punishment. You think you're punishing the people you hold grudges against, but that's usually not the case, especially when the grudge hangs on for some time. You're only punishing yourself. You waste a lot of energy being angry.

It teaches nothing. In no way does holding a grudge insure that the offender is going to learn some kind of lesson and behave better in the future—just because you withdrew your love and compassion from him or her.

Who we are and how we behave are not always the same. A person's essences and their behavior do not often mesh. That's because our behavior is a result of life experience, background, history, etc. When you can separate the essence from the actions, you're on the Dalai Lama trail. In life, people do the best they can, given the situation and the prevailing conditions.

Acceptance is the gateway to forgiveness. You have to see people beyond your expectations, and accept them, bad hair day and all. Nobody's perfect, nor should they have to be for you to accept and forgive them when they fail your expectations.

Don't let any non-forgivenesses linger. Make a list of the people you need to forgive and of the hurts that you want to heal.

Put your attention on the gifts of the relationship. Every relationship has positive elements. Dig in, decide what they are and write them down.

Communicate. If for some reason it isn't possible to meet face-to-face with the person who deserves forgiveness, write a letter. In extreme circumstances, maybe you don't mail this letter, but write it as if you will. Include in the letter what you value from your connection, and express sincere forgiveness.

Let it go. That's all there is to say. You've done the prep work, now let it go, move on.

Here's the bottom line: **Forgive easily, apologize immediately.** When someone else steps on your toes, forgiveness is divine. When you're the one doing the stepping, apologize.

Eileen Caddy, the founder of the Findhorn spiritual community in Scotland, says: *"Nothing really matters except what you do now in this instant of time. From this moment onwards you can be an entirely different person filled with love and understanding, ready with an outstretched hand, uplifted and positive in every thought and deed."*

"Holding a grudge is the same as drinking a tall glass of battery acid; both will corrode your insides."
—Tony Magee, MS, MBA

Seventeen Seemingly Simple Suggestions for Stopping or at least Slowing Stress

Stress is endemic in today's society. It affects every one of us in some way or the other. More than likely you're not going to eliminate stress. The question: what do you do when stress rears its toady little head? The answer: instead of buying into the stress, here are a few stress releasing suggestions.

Annual re-new-al vacation. At least once a year, go somewhere totally new, that you've never been to before.

Breathe. Fill your lungs, fill your belly with God's most precious gift. Breathe deeply, let go, let the breath do its work.

Celebrate your victories. Everyday, count your accomplishments, no matter how small. Make a list. Congratulate yourself. When you've done something noteworthy, reward yourself.

Change your diet. Diets that feature coffee, spicy foods and sugar are gold-plated invitations to stress and tension.

Change your sleep habits. Get a good night's sleep, and then get up early enough that you're not already behind, having to hurry-scurry your morning away.

Do one thing at a time. The ability to multi-task would seem to be the ticket to thriving in this day and age, but if it's causing you enough stress that you can't enjoy the fruits of your labor —what's the point?

Let go of being perfect. You don't have to do it all, know it all. Ask for help now and then.

Organize. Create a daily power hour in which you plan and strategize. You may be surprised how much stress is caused just by not having a decent blueprint for your life.

Pretend it's 100 years ago. Have an evening a week—or more if you can get away with it—with no TV, no CD, no DVD. (If you're really adventuresome, turn your telephone off.) Just you, and maybe your most relaxed buddy—if you have one—sitting, relaxing, reading.

Reach out more. Make time for your friends.

Surrender to nature. Commune with a tree, listen to the twirping of the birdies, smell the fresh air (assuming there is some where you live). Best of all, if it will let you—and unless it's sleeping, it probably won't—observe a cat for an hour. Cats are stress masters. Ask for a lesson.

Take a hike. Anywhere. Walk around the block, around your house, around your desk. Put your brains in your feet and move.

Take regular breaks. Stand, stretch, roll your shoulders, flex your fingers.

Take time for yourself. Spend some time alone every day. Make friends with silence.

Tell the truth. There's nothing more stressful than living a lie, big or little. And whatever truth you're holding back from others, is holding you back.

Tune into the present moment. Stress often lives in the past or the future, so when you fret about yesterday or worry about tomorrow, you invite stress to do a tap dance in your cranitorium. Look around.

Yes and No. Start saying yes—to yourself and your associates —for the things that you really love to do but don't allow enough. And start saying no to the things that you do for the wrong reasons.

Real Success

One of the most balanced individuals I ever had the pleasure of studying was Ralph Waldo Emerson. His personal vision for his life is reflected in his definition of success:

> *To laugh often and much;*
> *To win the respect of intelligent persons and the affection*
> *   of children;*
> *To earn the approval of honest critics and endure the*
> *   betrayal of false friends;*
> *To appreciate beauty;*
> *To find the best in others;*

To give of one's self without the slightest thought of return;
To have accomplished a task, whether by a healthy child,
    a rescued soul, a garden patch or a redeemed
    social condition;
To have played and laughed with enthusiasm and sung
    with exaltation;
To know that even one life has breathed easier because you
    have lived;
This is to have succeeded.

A Challenge for Your Summer

John Muir, the famous farmer, inventor, sheepherder, naturalist, explorer, writer, and conservationist once said *it was California's Sierra Nevada and Yosemite that truly claimed him.* In 1868, he walked across the San Joaquin Valley through waist-high wildflowers and into the high country for the first time. Later he would write: *"Then it seemed to me the Sierra should not be called the Nevada, or Snowy Range, but the Range of Light...the most divinely beautiful of all the mountain chains I have ever seen."* He herded sheep through that first summer and made his home in Yosemite.

    Muir said: *"Wander a whole summer, if you can. Thousands of God's wild blessings will search you and soak you as if you were a sponge and the big days will go by uncounted. If you are business tangled and so burdened by duty that only weeks can be got out of the heavy laden year, give a month at least. The time will not be taken from your sum of life. Instead of shortening it will indefinitely lengthen it and make you truly immortal. Nevermore will time seem short of long and cares will never again fall heavily on you, but gently and kindly as gifts from heaven."*

Charlie's Wobbly Chair

I have a friend that I visit periodically. Let's call him Charlie. Charlie and I sit around his kitchen table and talk about important things: our wives and kids, our work, our lives, the Lakers, basically, how the world works. For some reason I always end up sitting on the same wobbly chair. And then I always ask Charlie why he doesn't fix it. Charlie—a bit of a philosopher—always has the same answer: "That wobbly chair reminds me that you have to have all four legs for a well-balanced life." (Charlie's an astute thinker, but maybe a little lazy in the fix-it department.)

At which point, I find another chair to sit on. I don't think you need a defective chair to remind you, but Charlie's right. A great life has the same characteristics as a well-made four-legged chair. Each of the legs of a well-built chair must be strong enough to hold you up and be the same length, or like Charlie's chair, it will wobble. The same is true with a well-balanced life. To be the wonderful, destined life that you dream of, it must have equal amounts of four different elements: 1) *physical*, 2) *mental*, 3) *spiritual*, and 4) *financial*.

- **Physical:** you have to prioritize your body, exercise it, feed it well or all the plans you can make won't matter.

- **Mental:** keep sharp, challenge your mind, know your course and keep open to the unexpected.

- **Spiritual:** God—by any name or description —comes first. Your spiritual existence provides the fuel that powers your destiny.

- **Financial:** if you don't master the money game, you will waste time and energy trying to keep up.

I'm sure you know people who are about as balanced as Charlie's wobbly chair. How would you grade yourself? Which of your legs is the strongest? Which is the weakest? If you can hold the chair (that is your life) up to close inspection, you're on your way to creating a stronger state of balance.

I love him, but don't be like Charlie. Once you know why your chair wobbles, fix it!

Five Habits for Wellness

1. Believe that you can and must take good care of yourself. This is not selfishness.

2. Ask yourself often, What do I need to do right now to take better care of myself?

3. Tell yourself, I deserve the same kind of care I give other people. Then pay attention to your needs in the same way that you pay attention to friends, co-workers, and relatives.

4. Know what you need to do to season your routine with small pleasures. Adopt the philosophy that many of these small daily pleasures are only as far away as you make them.

5. Enjoy your life.

"Choose a job you love, and you will never have to work a day in you life."
        —Confucius

LIFE-ESSENTIAL TEN EXERCISE

How Well Would Your Life Wheel Roll You Around?

Together, the sixteen sections within the wheel below symbolize balance in your life! Grade the level of happiness for each life category—ranging from zero (the center of the wheel) to ten (the hub or wheel's outer edge.) Creating a new outer edge, draw a line with respect to the number you chose for that life section (**see example**). The new perimeter represents the wheel of your life. If this wheel were real, how well do you think you'd get around?

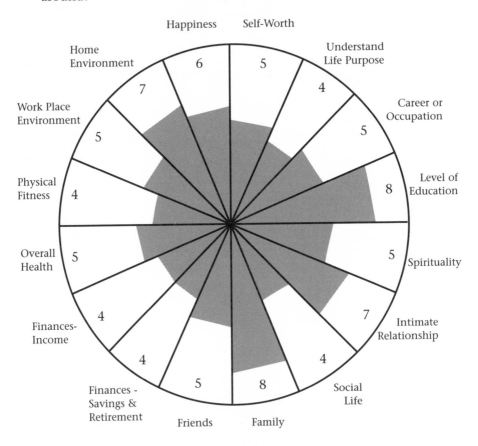

Example

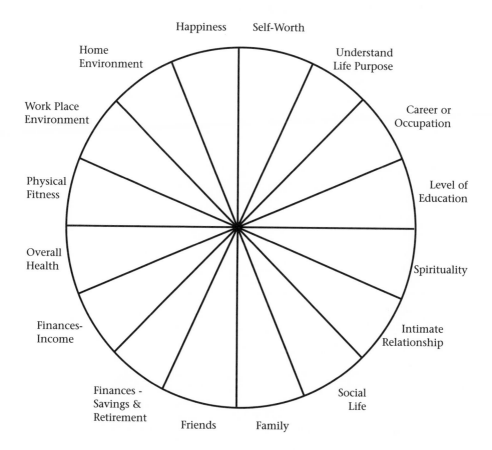

Exercise Questions: *Using What you Have Learned*

- Which three life categories did you score the highest?

- Which three life categories did you score the lowest?

- Take your top three life categories and list all your strengths that allowed you to score highest.

- Now, apply those same strengths to the areas in which you scored lowest. In time, you will see significant growth and improvement in those areas as well.

LIFE-ESSENTIAL  11

NOT BY OUR OWN BOOTSTRAPS

It Takes a Team to Fulfill a Dream

"No one of us got to where we are in life by pulling up our own bootstraps; someone bent down and helped us!"
—Thurgood Marshall

The Way of the Beaver

Beavers are more than just intriguing animals with flat tails, big teeth and lustrous fur. Native Americans often referred to the beaver's village as the "sacred center" of their land, because beavers construct valuable wildlife habitats. These animals live up to their reputation of being as "busy as a beaver." They dam streams, creating ponds that support fish, frogs, turtles, water-fowl, muskrats, minks, otters, and moose. Trees drowned by the rising water provide nest sites for woodpeckers, tree swallows, ospreys, and herons. Over time, the ponds fill in with sediment and become wet meadows for deer, elk, rabbits, and moles. Almost half of the endangered and threatened species in North America depend on wetlands, and the beaver's environment is a vital part of this.

As a part of nature's cycle, the beaver's tree cutting and

pruning stimulates willows to grow back bushier than ever the next spring. Beavers often use the peeled sticks to build teepee-like lodges (houses) on the shore and/or dams in the water. By damming streams, they raise the water level to surround their lodges with protective moats, at the same time guaranteeing the deep water needed for winter food storage. While other wildlife must endure the cold winters with hunger, the beaver stays nice and warm in its lodge, with a nearby underwater food cache.

Why are beavers so intriguing? What makes them a champion species? What can we learn from the way of the beaver? I'll tell you what it is in a word: teamwork. It's their professional and systematic way of working together without getting on each other's nerves and in each other's way. Wildlife experts report beavers to be gentle, reasoning beings that maintain positive attitudes. Normally, you'll see a colony of six or more beavers working together.

If you spotted a half a dozen beavers in a stream building a damn,—do you think you could point out the leader within the team? Probably not, because before you arrived, they would likely have already finished their staff meeting. Instead you'd see a bunch of look-alike beavers working together doing different tasks to accomplish the dam construction. This is what makes them so special. During their staff meeting, the leader beaver would have assessed the talents of each beaver in the cluster and then coupled that specific talent to a specific task. This is why you'll see one beaver gathering smaller branches, another collecting larger ones, one beaver hauling mud, another bringing leaves, one assisting anyone who needs it, and another assembling the dam. The *way of the beaver* presents a valuable lesson: *a team working cooperatively together will achieve their common dream or goal.*

Once a Penny Stock

By the beginning of the twelfth grade, I knew it was time to prepare for my freshman year in college. Applications were due and I had to get ready for my SATs. My grades were pretty good, but I didn't quite have all of the necessary course requirements to get into engineering school. Yes, I had completed all of the general subjects—like history, government, English literature, physical education, earth science, and art. However, the highest level of math that I had studied was only geometry—not to mention that I had never taken any chemistry or physics. Nevertheless, my mind was set on going to college and somehow getting into engineering school.

To make this happen, I solicited help from three teachers at Westchester High; my goal was to train my brain to pass the college entrance exams. I've heard others say that *the teacher will appear when the student is ready*—boy was I ready! Mr. Brian Kataoka—my math teacher—trained me in math. Mr. Mario Tan—my science teacher—prepared me for chemistry and physics. Mrs. Margaret Bower—my art teacher—helped me improve my writing skills so I could pass the English placement portion of the exam. All of my college preparation occurred within six months before finally being accepted to a university.

I had little money on my side, so I needed financial assistance for tuition, food, and housing. Luckily I was one of Mrs. Bower's favorite art students. She decided to invite me over for dinner one evening to meet her husband, Larry, and their four children, Justin, Erin, Ann, and Mary. The Bowers lived in Hermosa Beach, a suburban seaside community south of Los Angeles. Their beautiful home had an awesome view of the Pacific Ocean. It was as though *Ozzie & Harriet* had moved to *Fantasy Island*—certainly nothing I'd ever experienced. After a full course meal—which included broccoli fettuccini Alfredo, tossed salad, roasted Italian chicken, and homemade chocolate cake—my stomach was full and I was too happy. Mr. Bower took the time to review my college and financial aid applications to make sure everything was in order. Before the night was over, he said, *Margaret, I really like this kid. He's going to go far in life—really far. I say we adopt him.* And they did. They call me "Son" and we've been a family ever since 1986.

In college, two wonderful women sustained what my high school mentors had begun. These women went out of their way to continue to make things happen for me while I was attending California State University, Northridge (CSUN). Margaret June Brown was a well-known academic advisor who had looked out for my cousin Darryl Claiborne when he had attended CSUN a decade earlier. She kindly agreed to do the same for me. Ms. Brown helped me secure my course schedule, financial aid and housing. Gigi Littlejohn-McGuire was my other "shero" who served as a recruiter for the Minority Engineering Program at CSUN. Gigi strategically got me conditionally accepted into the School of Engineering for one year while I completed all of the prerequisites for full acceptance. She told me: *Tony, your positive attitude and enthusiasm for learning are more important in recruiting you than your transcripts. A lot of folks have the transcripts, but won't have the guts to finish the race. My bet is that you're not only going to finish—you're going to pass many at the grandstand. I believe in you!* In one year, I made a quantum leap from geometry to calculus—from literally no real science to college chemistry and physics. My self-esteem was running on high.

Now, all I needed was a fine example to model myself after. I wanted a professor who would show me how to be an engineer—how to think, walk, talk, and dress like one. During my second year, it happened for me. Dr. Behzad Bavarian was not only my teacher; he became my mentor, friend, father figure, and lifetime advisor. Dr. B. would always say to me, *Tony Magee, you will never be defeated!* I believed anything he said. With his unconventional style of teaching, through the principles of discipline and preparedness, I found untapped excellence that would allow me to finish my undergraduate education and go on to earn two master degrees—one in engineering and the other in business. My relationship with Dr. Bavarian was like *Tuesdays With Morrie*, Mitch Albom's book about his relationship with his old college professor Morrie Schwartz.

Each one of the aforementioned people chose to help a challenged young person up out of his mud. They all invested their time and money in me. They recognized that I was just like a *penny stock*—an undervalued gem that would bring an excellent return on their investment!

"You must network with quality people to help fulfill your dreams! The key to networking is not necessarily what you know, or whom you know. It's who knows you!"
　　　—Otis "Limitless" Williams

Hitsville USA

What does Mickey D's (McDonald's), The Ford Motor Company, and Mr. Berry Gordy, Jr. all have in common? They're all experts at mass production and quality control. Berry Gordy learned how to create and mass produce a quality product while working for McDonald's as a young adult and later as an upholstery cutter on the assembly line at Henry Ford's company. In pursuit of his dream and truest love—music—Berry Gordy applied the science of mass production to the field of entertainment. In the process, he created one of the largest black-owned business in America and more significantly, he forever changed the face and sound of American popular music.

Born and raised during the Great Depression, Gordy was the seventh of eight children. His family lived in the tough Detroit Lower East Side ghetto, so life was not a piece of cake for the youngster. Known as the impetuous one, he often had great ideas that could never quite come to fruition.

Gordy first wanted to become a boxer. Joe Louis was his first real source of inspiration. In the 1930s, Louis was the Heavyweight Champion of the World, the American Idol. "The Brown Bomber" had just handily defeated Germany's Heavy Weight Champion Max Schmelling,—Adolf Hitler's poster boy for the so-called "master race." Joe Louis was beloved by black kids all across America.

Gordy was pretty good with his hands, and he did manage to do a short stint as a professional fighter. Once he even fought on the same boxing card as his hero Joe Louis. But Gordy soon realized that he'd never become another Louis. So he considered another form of entertainment instead. That was music. According to H.W. Brand, author of *Masters of Enterprise*, Gordy had an epiphany after an especially tiresome workout in the summer of 1950. He noticed two posters on one of the four square pillars that held up the boxing gym's ceiling. The first poster advertised a "Battle of the Bands" between Stan Kenton and Duke Ellington. Just below it, the second poster announced a boxing match between two fighters. He realized that the musicians had a steady means of getting paid and were having fun. And he also understood that a prizefighter could fight one time, get seriously hurt and never fight again. The funniest thing he considered was that the boxers were in their twenties and looked fifty; while the band leaders were in their fifties and looked to be in their twenties. Gordy decided quickly that a career in music might be more lucrative and less physically harmful!

To pursue his new dream, Gordy wrote songs in his spare time and visited nightclubs to listen to and learn about his passion—music. In 1957, he and his good boxing-buddy Jackie Wilson co-wrote a few hits together, including *Lonely Teardrops.* Although they produced many hits songs, they made very little money! All of the proceeds would end up in the pockets of the key executives who owned the record company. While building a solid reputation as a successful songwriter, Gordy became more and more miserable working for someone else. Smokey Robinson, lead singer of the Miracles, convinced Gordy to record and distribute his own music. Along with his song-writing, Gordy had already produced acts like The Miracles for record companies.

In 1959, twenty-nine-year-old Berry Gordy, Jr., took out an $800 loan from his family and started a record company. Even getting this family money wasn't that easy. Some time earlier, Gordy's parents had established a savings fund into which they and their adult children contributed $10 per month. Individual family members might borrow money from the fund—*but only with the approval of the contributors.* Although his mother and father were inclined to approve Gordy's $800 with-drawal, his sister Esther wanted some kind of proof that the money would not be wasted. His sister asked Gordy, *what he had done so far in his life?* All that Gordy could respectfully say in return was that he had a dream he believed in.

Even with that answer, Esther was more concerned about the $800 than her brother's dream. After giving him a hard time, she finally signed off only after he promised his future royalties as collateral against the loan.

Gordy set up his musical headquarters in a dilapidated bungalow squeezed in between a funeral home and a beauty parlor in a poor Detroit neighborhood. The building entrance was adorned with a big sign that oddly bragged *"Hitsville USA."* The kitchen functioned as the control room, the garage became the two-track studio, the living room was reserved for book-keeping, and product marketing and sales were handled in the dining room. Word rapidly spread around town that any young person with a trace of talent should visit the only record label that Detroit had seen in years. The company would be called *Motown Records*. Gordy knew that every new company needed a niche to get going in business. Since Detroit was known as the *motor* city, he played on its notoriety and came up with *Motown*.

Gordy's goal was to produce popular music with soul that his crossover customers would purchase. Gordy presumed that if whites would buy black music performed by whites such as Elvis Presley and others, then they might be persuaded to buy black music performed by blacks. His timing was good as racial barriers were being shaken. Segregation was starting to dwindle.

Uncertain of where his dreams might lead, Gordy knew he needed to surround himself with a highly creative, dynamic and diverse team. He summoned the songwriting talents of his friend Smokey Robinson. Smokey had come to Gordy with a notebook full of songs, a smooth crooning voice, and unshakable ambition. Without Smokey, Motown might have never earned the boasted title of Hitsville USA.

Once referred to as America's greatest living poet, Smokey Robinson wrote nearly thirty Top 40 hits with his group The Miracles. He co-wrote and produced such unforgettable songs as *"My Girl"* for the Temptations and *"My Guy"* for Mary Wells. Smokey created some of the most memorable and romantic pop songs. He wrote and performed the tunes *"Ooo Baby Baby," "The Way You Do The Things You Do," "The Tracks of My Tears," "You've Really Got a Hold On Me," "Tears of a Clown,"* and *"I Second That Emotion."*

Gordy gathered the most talented team of musicians during the 1960s. Commonly known as The Funk Brothers, these remarkable rhythm and blues masters powered the new sound of America's young people. They were masterful musicians from Detroit, submerged as deeply in modern jazz as they were in rhythm and blues. The Funk Brothers' stimulating rhythms delivered countless smash hits by the Temptations, Smokey Robinson & the Miracles, Diana Ross & the Supremes, Stevie Wonder, and many other top acts of the Motown '60s.

To deal with a racially sensitive entertainment industry, Gordy hired a professional team of nearly all white sales and marketing representatives—some of the best talent that money could buy. Gordy's business savvy and strategy helped to remove barriers between blacks and whites, as well as R&B and Pop categories. He also partnered with a team of experts in the fields of charm and etiquette, choreography, vocal coaching, costume design, photography, and asset management. *Hitsville* became a one-stop-shop where rough jewels would be polished into platinum stars.

Over a decade, from 1960 to 1970, Motown released 535 singles and 357 of them were hits! This two-third ratio was better than twice the record industry's average. Berry Gordy's secret to producing hit records was his famous *sandwich test.* He would determine if a particular blend of melody and lyrics would sell by asking this simple question—*Would you buy this record for a dollar or would you buy a sandwich?* This turned out to be a brilliant business strategy that identified musical winners.

With superstar talents ranging from Gladys Knight & the Pips to the Four Tops, from Marvin Gaye to the Jackson Five & Little Michael Jackson, from the Commodores to Rick James & Teena Marie, Motown became a household name and remarkable record label. Thanks to Berry Gordy's creative vision, and the assemblage of his dream team, *Hitsville USA* became one of the greatest icons of music in American history and culture.

I wanted to include a comprehensive view of Berry Gordy because he was a big part of my childhood. Like a cousin or an uncle, Berry was an extended member of my family. Not in a physical form, but in the form of the hundreds of Motown records that we owned. Back in the seventies, I remember having dozens of little forty-five-RPM records with those little yellow discs pressed inside the center hole—spread all over the living room floor. I can still see those different colored record labels, which were the blue and white *Motown*, brown and yellow *Tamla*, and purple and gold *Gordy.*

I knew at a very early age that Berry Gordy came from the humblest of beginnings, challenged by scarcity and misery. And I knew that he had a burning desire to live his dream out loud, to become a master of enterprise. Berry Gordy faced my life in the right direction; he was a shining example of what I could do if my mind was set on success. *Thank you, Mr. Gordy.*

"No one can whistle a symphony. It takes a whole orchestra to play."

—H. E. Luccock

"It has never been my object to record my dreams, just the determination to realize them."

—Man Ray

Time, Money & Mind Synergy

I often hear people say, *Time is money*. Time and money are very important, but are not synonyms. Time is *not* money. In fact, time is more precious than money. When you lose money, you can always retrieve more. When you lose your time, it's gone forever. This is why we should be aware of our time and how it is spent. We have to choose the people we spend our time with carefully. People must meet certain qualifications for you to be willing to spend your time on them. Time is not money—time is your life. Never again ask yourself, *Is it worth my time?* Instead ask, *Is it worth my life?*

Napoleon Hill once said, *No one rises above mediocrity that does not learn to use the brains of other people. And sometimes the money of other people as well*. Yes, in order to fulfill your dreams, you must secure a team. You can't do it alone. You have to become an expert selector of other individuals who will become assets to you and your vision. Selecting the members of your dream team, as you would choose your fruit—polished without ugly spots. And remember that no one will accomplish his or her goals without benefiting others within the dream team.

There are two advantages to surrounding yourself with a dream team. The first is *efficiency*; you can do more together and you can do it better than you would alone. The second is *collective brainpower*. Do you remember the old adage—*two heads are better than one?* If we connect our brainpower with other efficient minds in a spirit of cooperation—this will produce more thinking energy than any one mind could alone.

"There are two kinds of people in this world—battery drainers and battery chargers. If you were a battery, what group would you care to be around?"

—Aloria Lei Magee, M.Ed.

Three Vee & Successful Dream-Teams

The name of this book is *Can't Shove a Great Life into a Small Dream*. You have to dream big. And once you have decided on your biggest dream, know this: if the dream is as big as it should be, you can't do it alone. You need to create a *Dream-Team* to make it happen. About the best Dream-Team example I can think of is a film company aptly named *DreamWorks SKG*. It was founded in October 1994 by three noteworthy gentlemen, all successful in their own right. Steven Spielberg is the famed film director/producer, Jeffrey Katzenberg the former chairman of Disney Studios and animation guru, and David Geffen, the recording industry maven. They could have rested on their laurels or just continued on their individual life paths, but they had a bigger dream. Upon inception, they announced plans to launch film, music, software, and television projects.

DreamWorks SKG is now a leading producer of live-action motion pictures; animated feature films; network, syndicated, and cable television programming; home video and DVD entertainment; and consumer goods. Some of the mega productions that their brainchild has created are *Shrek, Saving Private Ryan, Antz, The Peacemaker, Amistad, American Beauty, Gladiator, Chicken Run, The Legend of Bagger Vance, The Mexican, Biker Boyz, The Road to Perdition, The Ring,* and *Catch Me If You Can*.

Not everything they've produced has been successful — after all, the movie and TV business is a fickle mistress—but DreamWorks SKG is without doubt a mega-hitter in the industry and is unquestionably fulfilling its Dream-Team mandate.

For the record, let me cite a few other examples of successful Dream-Teams: Microsoft and NBC, Disney and ABC, Daimler-Chrysler, Helen Keller and Johanna "Anne" Sullivan, Jimmy Jam and Terry Lewis, the late Don Simpson and Jerry Bruckheimer, Kenneth "Babyface" Edmonds and Antonio "L.A." Reid, and Lucille Ball and Dezi Arnaz. (I would like to include AOL Time Warner in this list, but as of this writing, the jury is still out on this marriage.)

As I studied the power of the Dream-Team phenomena, I saw that at the heart of every successful alliance, there are three key ingredients, which I call *Three Vee: Vision, Variety, and Value*. (With his hand in the air in a stubborn victory sign, it could be said that Winston Churchill was the *One Vee* man. Richard Nixon one-upped him by using both hands, so let's call him the *Two Vee* man. I'm the *Three Vee* man—although, without an extra hand, I haven't figured out how to make a Three Vee sign. Another reason why I need a team to stream my dream.)

Vision: First and foremost, there has to be vision. A team has to gather around a purpose, a mission, a sense of direction. The DreamWorks moguls came together because they had a strong idea of what they wanted to create, and regardless of how powerful they were individually, they knew they couldn't pull it off alone. This word—Vision—is bandied around a lot in self-help circles and in the motivational arena, and there is a good reason for that. The journey towards dream fulfillment starts here. Vision is the maypole around which a team gathers. Without a strong vision, the team doesn't know which way to face, or even what their individual roles might be.

Variety: This second principal accentuates the power in diversity, the condition of accessing different points of reference. When there is an emphasis on variety, it's much easier to maintain an open mind and allow other people's opinions. Spielberg, Katzenberg and Geffen—and the myriad of key players that surround them—thrive in an atmosphere of variety. Once a Dream-Team is gathered around a strong sense of purpose, variety is the spice of success. If you're truly committed to go for your dream, you don't want to be surrounded by *Yes-men and women*. Seek out people who can support your vision, but who bring opinions and strategies that add to the mix, instead of just echoing what everyone else is saying. When there is adequate variety within your team, it's much easier to assist one another in your common endeavors—sharing your strengths and compensating for each other's weaknesses.

Somewhere or another I heard that hell is a place where

everyone thinks exactly the same way you do. Don't create a Dream-Team from hell. Make sure there is sufficient variety.

Value: As much as any other factor, DreamWorks SKG was created because its founders had need to achieve a particular kind of value. Their big dream was to create an artist-friendly studio to develop, produce, and distribute superior film and music entertainment that would inspire and delight audiences worldwide. Within the film studio world, they wanted to give value. It's one thing to sell a product or service, it's quite another to add value. As you gather your Dream-Team, I strongly suggest that you place as much emphasis on adding value as you do to establishing vision.

The *Three Vees—Vision, Variety* and *Value*—work so well as a team. Vision asks the question: *What are we doing?* Variety asks: *Who is doing it?* Value asks: *How are we doing it?*

Let's take the example of a supermarket.

Vision... The over-riding purpose of a supermarket is to make groceries available to their customers. Each department must be aimed in the same direction for the store to fulfill its mandate and be profitable. There is no way a supermarket could function unless everyone involved understood this. (Now that I think about it, I've been in some stores where I'm not sure they all did understand this. I remember a clerk in a neighborhood market who must have thought giving astrological advice was a lot more important than ringing up sales.)

Variety... There has to be a variety of interests and talent. The supermarket wouldn't function if everyone was a cashier. Who would stock the shelves, tend to the produce, service the bakery and meat departments? Moreover, who would manage the store? Diversity—centered around a common purpose—is absolutely necessary for the supermarket to function.

Value... It's one thing to sell groceries, it's quite another to make the customer feel special, to give that extra something that is so memorable. We're living in such a techno-quickie age, the human touch can get totally lost in the shuffle. I can buy groceries anywhere, but I remember and appreciate the value, the special attention that comes along with the groceries. The main focus of any successful business is to delight the customer. (Let me be clear here, I have nothing against the Zodiak, but I don't think mini-astrology readings at the check-out counter really adds value.)

"Fulfilling your dreams lies in your ability to create extraordinary partnerships!"
—Tony Magee, MS, MBA

Let There Be Light

Thomas Alva Edison was both a scientist and an inventor. He would see tremendous change take place in his lifetime. Edison was also responsible for making many of those changes happen. When Edison was just a baby boy, society still thought electricity was too new to be taken seriously. Before Thomas Edison died, cities all over the world had been illuminated by electricity. His most famous invention was an incandescent light bulb. It's a little known fact that if it were not for one member of his dream team, the light bulb might have been too impractical for most people to use. One of Edison's most valuable partners was Lewis Howard Latimer, who is considered a renaissance man because of his talent as a brilliant inventor and electrical engineer, but he was also a poet, playwright, and visual artist.

It was Latimer's work that helped make possible the widespread use of electric lights—quite an achievement for this son of parents who escaped the bondage of slavery. Latimer developed and patented the method for making carbon filaments used in electric lamps. Thomas Edison's light bulb used bamboo as the filament and the light bulb burned out after only thirty hours. Latimer knew carbon lasted much longer, which made the light bulb practical and profitable.

Lewis Latimer was hired on at the Edison Electric Light Company as an inventor and patent expert. Today the company is called General Electric (GE). Latimer was the only black member of Edison's Pioneers—Thomas Alva Edison's elite team of inventors. Edison was wise to make Latimar a key member of the team.

Betcha Can't Eat Just One

In the fall of 1932, Elmer Doolin stopped at a little eatery in San Antonio, Texas. He ordered an ordinary sandwich, which cost about five cents back in those days. While patiently waiting for his sandwich to be made, he glanced over on the countertop and saw plain unmarked packages of corn chips. Curious, Doolin decided to spend another nickel for a package of the funny-looking yellow chips. Doolin had no idea that this five-cent exchange would deliver the inspiration for an entire company! This delicious handmade snack was made from corn mesa, an ingredient which had been used for hundreds of years in bread products by Mexicans living in the Southwest.

Doolin's primary business was selling ice cream, however a price war had broken out with other sellers. What he needed was another type of food product to sell—something revolutionary. By 1938, he located the maker of the tasty corn snacks; and the gentleman was ready and willing to sell the recipe. Doolin negotiated the deal for $100—money that he borrowed from close associates. After acquiring the red-hot recipe, Doolin landed nineteen retail accounts.

At first, the new corn snacks were made in the kitchen of Mrs. Daisy Doolin—Elmer's mother. Originally the chips had been referred to by a rather long Mexican name, but Doolin used only its root—Frito—to come up with the brand name *Fritos®*. Early production runs were about ten to twelve pounds daily. This resulted in an average of nine dollars income per day, and Doolin would clear maybe two or three dollars profit. He prepared the Fritos at night and sold them during the daytime out of his car, a trusted Ford Model T.

With his new business venture, Elmer Doolin would soon experience a dilemma. His sales had increased, requiring more room for production to satisfy the demand. Doolin created a new hand-operated food press machine that would replace what they had been using—an old potato ricer. Eventually, the operation was upgraded, including the packaging. Doolin moved his operations from San Antonio to Dallas, which was the city of the future for big business in the Southwest.

Simultaneously—while Elmer Doolin was establishing The Frito Company in Southwest—a different kind of snack chip was gaining popularity throughout the Southeast. Another entrepreneur had started a potato chip manufacturing company out of Nashville, Tennessee. His name was Herman W. Lay.

Herman Lay, like Elmer Doolin, also distributed snack chips from his car—a Ford Model A. Lay had originally started out distributing potato chips and other snack foods for an Atlanta-based manufacturer. In 1938, that company experienced financial problems that jeopardized Lay's supply of snacks. Ambitiously, with the help of his friends and close business associates, Lay purchased the company and named it H.W. Lay & Company.

Lay returned the profits to his business and it rapidly expanded. With *Lay's®* brand potato chips being their primary cash cow, H.W. Lay & Company became a primary snack food operation in the Southeast. Meanwhile, the Frito Company was achieving comparable success with its Fritos brand corn chips.

In 1942, World War II caused a delay in business expansion for both The Frito Company and H.W. Lay & Company. Still Fritos remained a favorite snack chip of the Southwest, and Lay's potato chips ruled the Southeast. By 1945, The Frito Company offered an earlier franchise of their corn chips to H.W. Lay & Company, so Frito could be sold throughout the Southeast. This initial move helped the two expanding companies develop a relationship.

By 1959, Frito brand corn chips had become the leading snack food in all of America, and that same year Elmer Doolin died. In September 1961, twenty-nine years after two individual dreams were simultaneously born, The Frito Company and H.W. Lay & Company merged and became Frito-Lay, Inc. Though Doolin and Lay had both started their individual businesses with roughly $100 each, their dreams came together to become one of the most profitable snack food companies in the world— worth more than $20 billion today. Both businesses were originally built on a simple philosophy: *Make the best product possible; sell it at a fair price; and make service a fundamental part of doing business.* Whenever you decide to eat any of their many products: Fritos, Ruffles, Cheetos, Doritos, Tostitos, Munchos, Funyons, Santitas, Rold Gold Pretzels, or Lay's potato chips — *betcha can't eat just one!*

"The way a team plays as a whole determines its success. You may have the greatest bunch of individual stars in the world, but if they don't play together, the club won't be worth a dime."
—Babe Ruth

Now, to help you build your dream team, answer the following questions and then read on.

LIFE-ESSENTIAL ELEVEN EXERCISE

You can begin identifying your dream team by answering the following:

1. Is your life filled with diverse people who are committed to a common goal or dream? If so, who are they?

2. Have you surrounded yourself with a team of traveling companions who include as one of their priorities your well-being? If so, who are they?

3. Do your relationships uplift you and move you along the road to success? If so, in what way?

4. List the names of five to eight individuals whom you would desire to be a part of your dream team. Also, state why these people would be an asset for you to achieve your goals or dream.

LIFE-ESSENTIAL 12

READ ANY GOOD BOOKS LATELY?

Great Readers Make Greater Leaders

"Reading is FUN-damental!"

—Anonymous

This chapter contains my personal book list. These powerful books can help you discover and release your untapped potential. I hope that this personal list of books will initiate a chain reaction that will unearth your unique gifts and lead you to bona fide success. My mother always said, "If you want to keep anything from the ignorant, just put it in a book—because ignorant folk don't read!" She certainly was not referring to you.

My aim with *Can't Shove a Great Life into a Small Dream* has been to introduce you to exceedingly effective techniques used by successful people—and, of course, my own techniques are included.

The majority of the titles on this list are relatively newer releases, although some of the books I recommend are old and out of print. Nevertheless, they are as relevant to you and your life today as they were to others in days past. You should be able to find the older books in used bookstores, as well as local and university libraries.

I urge you to appreciate the value of each book. I advise that you read, study and apply the principles in personal and professional development books, as well as workbooks, magazines, and news journals. And it's equally important to share your knowledge and wisdom with others. Sharing is actually a win/win situation—for while you're giving the information away, you still get to keep it for yourself!

There's an art to reading books for personal and professional development. First, ascertain *what you are searching for* before you start reading. If you know what you are looking for, you will be more apt to find it than will the many people who do not read with a purpose in mind. Then you must *concentrate* as you read. Each author is trying to convey his or her secrets to success. While reading, assume that the author is a close friend of yours and wrote their book just for you. Take the time while reading to stop and reflect on all the life-changing principles.

I recommend that you read personal and professional development books four times. Each pass will have a different purpose. Here are the four phases:

1. **Read for general subject matter:** This is your first read-through. Just read the book quickly to get a snapshot of what is to be learned. However, do take the time to highlight important ideas during your first run. Use the margins to jot down notes (you never know if you'll get a second chance to do so). Notations within your books make them more valuable to you during re-reads.

2. **Read for specific emphasis:** Read the second time around to incorporate some of the specific ideas important to your life situation today. During this reading, it's important for you to try to master these portions of the material.

3. **Read for your future:** Reading a book for the third time is important for memorizing specific portions that will be valuable to you in the future. Find ways to relate the memorized selections to issues that you're likely to have to work through. Just study the good stuff and pass on the rest.

4. **Read again later to recharge your memory and to be inspired all over again:** No batteries last forever—not even the pink bunny's. They may keep going and going, but eventually the charge will run out. Batteries either have to be recharged or thrown out. We're the same. Sometime we get drained and need to be recharged or inspired to go on. We should re-read the best of our books at such times to rekindle the flames that got us going in the earlier rounds.

"A man who carries a book of wisdom around without reading it is no better than a camel that carries that same book on its back. In fact, the man is worse, because camels can't read."
—Tony Magee MS, MBA

Below I've listed some of the greatest personal and professional development books; I promise that these books can inspire you to live your best life. All of them contain pearls of wisdom for your personal discovery. But before you move on to this wonderful bibliography—thank you for finishing Can't Shove a Great Life into a Small Dream! (If you haven't finished my book, and just skipped to this bibliography, go back and dive into the unread portions before you start on another book.)

Remember, great leaders are great readers. Happy reading to you!

Zig Ziglar
See You At the Top
Over the Top

Napoleon Hill
Think and Grow Rich
The Law of Success
Success Through a Positive Mental Attitude
(with W. Clement Stone)

Elwood N. Chapman
Attitude: Your Most Priceless Possession
Life Is an Attitude

Dan Clark
Puppies for Sale

Don Hutson, *Chris Crouch & George Lucas*
The Contented Achiever

Stephen R. Covey
First Things First
The 7 Habits of Highly Effective People

Wynn Davis
The Best of Success

Adam Smith
The Wealth of Nations

Shad Helmsetter, Ph.D.
What to Say When You Talk to Yourself

Jack Canfield & Mark Victor Hansen
Chicken Soup for the Soul Series
The Aladdin Factor
Dare To Win

Mark Victor Hansen & Robert G. Allen
The One Minute Millionaire

Peter McWilliams
You Can't Afford the Luxury of a Negative Thought

David J. Schwartz, Ph.D.
The Magic of Thinking Big

Dr. Norman Vincent Peale
You Can If You Think You Can
The Power of Positive Thinking
Enthusiasm Makes the Difference

Bishop T.D. Jakes
Maximize the Moment
The Lady, Her Lover, and Her Lord
God's Leading Lady

Og Mandino
The Greatest Salesman in the World

James Allen
As a Man Thinketh

George S. Clason
The Richest Man in Babylon

Robert T. Kiyosaki
Rich Dad Poor Dad
Rich Dad's Cashflow Quadrant

Bishop Kenneth C. Ulmer
Spiritually Fit to Run the Race

John Alston & Lloyd Thaxton
Stuff Happens

Willie Jolley
It Only Takes a Minute to Change Your Life!
A Setback Is a Setup for a Comeback

Don Miguel Ruiz
The Four Agreements

Bill Cohen
Life Mapping

Sam Horn
Tongue Fu
Take the Bully by the Horns

Terry Paulsen, Ph.D.
Paulsen on Change
50 Tips for Speaking Like a Pro

Dr. Phillip C. McGraw
Self Matters
Relationship Rescue

Max DePree
Leadership is an Art

Margaret J. Wheatley
Leadership and the New Science

John Steinbeck
The Pearl

Les Brown
Live Your Dreams
It's Not Over Until You Win

Dr. Dennis Kimbro
Think and Grow Rich: A Black Choice

Kelvin Boston
Smart Money Moves for African Americans

Jerrold Mundis
How to Get Out of Debt, Stay Out of Debt & Live Prosperously

Dottie & Lilly Walters
Speak and Grow Rich

Suze Orman
The 9 Steps to Financial Freedom
The Courage to Be Rich

Stedman Graham
You Can Make It Happen
Build Your Own Life Brand!

Albert Mensah
When the Drumbeat Changes, Dance a Different Dance

Rene Godefroy
No Condition Is Permanent!

Marilyn Sherman
Whose Comfort Zone Are You In?

Zonya Foco
Lickety-Split Meals for Health Conscious People on the Go!

Dr. Wayne W. Dyer
Manifest Your Destiny
There's a Spiritual Solution to Every Problem
10 Secrets for Success and Inner Peace

Ian Percy
Going Deep

Carolyn Kalil
Follow Your True Colors to the Work You Love

Ben Carson, M.D.
Think Big (with Cecil Murphy)
Gifted Hands

H.W. Brand
Masters of Enterprise

Thomas J. Stanley, Ph.D. & William D. Danko, Ph.D.
The Millionaire Next Door

Carol Adrienne
The Purpose of Your Life

Earl Nightingale
The Strangest Secret
Lead the Field (Audio Set)

Brian Tracy
Create Your Own Future
Victory!
Focal Point
The Psychology of Achievement (Audio Set)
Maximum Achievement

Denis Waitley
Seeds of Greatness
The Psychology of Winning (Audio Set)

Iyanla Vanzant
Acts of Faith

Dale Carnegie
How to Win Friends and Influence People

Michael E. Gerber
The E-Myth

His Holiness The Dalai Lama
& Howard C. Cutler, M.D.
The Art of Happiness: A Handbook for Living

Patricia Fripp
Get What You Want

Jack Barnard
We Get Our Cue From You

Tony Magee, MS, MBA
Can't Shove a Great Life into a Small Dream

Keith D. Harrell
Attitude Is Everything

Gary Zukav
The Seat of the Soul

Khalil Gabran
The Prophet

Eknath Easwaran
Your Life Is Your Message

Alex Haley
Roots
The Autobiography of Malcolm X

Richard Wright
Black Boy

Dr. Robert Anthony
The Ultimate Secrets of Total Self-Confidence

Dr. Nathaniel Branden
The Six Pillars of Self-Esteem
How to Raise Your Self-Esteem

Marcia Steele
Making It in America

Cornelius A. DeKluyver
Strategic Thinking

Viktor E. Frankl
Man's Search for Meaning

Mary-Ellen Drummond
Fearless and Flawless Public Speaking

James MacGregor Burns
Leadership

Frank & P. Bunny Wilson
The Master's Degree: Majoring in Your Marriage

Nido Qubein
Stairway to Success
How to Be a Great Communicator

Otis Williams
Victory 4 Youth! Succeeding Against the Odds

Ona Brown
Affirmacise! A Fitness Gym for the Mind & Spirit

Jonathan Sprinkles
Why Settle? Be The Best You That You Can Be

John C. Maxwell
Failing Forward
Leadership 101

Bruce Wilkinson
The Prayer of Jabez

James M. Kouzes & Barry Z. Posner
Encouraging the Heart

Stanley Bing
What Would Machiavelli Do?

Throwing the Elephant: Managing and the Art of Managing Up

Susan L. Taylor
In the Spirit

Maya Angelou
The Complete Collected Poems of Maya Angelou
I Know Why the Caged Bird Sings
Gather Together in My Name

Larry Winget
How to Write a Book: One Page at a Time

Mary LoVorde
Stop Screaming at the Microwave

Susan Jeffers
Feel the Fear and Do It Anyway

Marcia Wieder
Making Your Dreams Come True

Deepak Chopra, MD
The Seven Spiritual Laws of Success

Tony Robbins
Awaken the Giant Within
Unlimited Power

Art Berg
Some Miracles Take Time
The Impossible Just Takes a Little Longer

Harvey McKay
Shark Proof
Swim with Sharks without Being Eaten Alive
Dig Your Well Before You're Thirsty
Pushing the Envelope

WANT TO LEARN MORE?

For information on:

Keynote Speaking
Organizational Coaching & Consulting
Personal Development Coaching
Life-Essentials™ Workshops & Events

By Tony Magee, MS, MBA

Call us at:
866-ASK-TONY
(866-275-8669)

Or go online at:
www.platinumstar.com

PlatinumStar™ Performance Systems

PlatinumStar aims to motivate and encourage everyday people to unleash their human potential personally and professionally, and inspire them to live their best lives through uplifting books, powerful seminars and keynotes, and peak performance consulting.

Consulting clients include *American Red Cross, United Way, Chevron-Texaco, The Boeing Company, Bloomingdales, The Target Corporation, CostCo.,* among others.

Visit us today at:
www.platinumstar.com

I'd Love
to Hear from You!

I'd be elated to know what Life-Essential™ strategies work for you. Please send me your ideas, insights, feedback, and stories. Contact me at:

Tony Magee, MS, MBA

PlatinumStar™ Performance Systems

PO Box 891

Woodland Hills, CA 91365-0891

866-ASK-TONY / 866-275-8669

818-992-6443 Fax

tony@platinumstar.com

www.platinumstar.com

Can't Shove a Great Life into a Small Dream™

Item	Unit Cost	Quantity	Total
Book	$19.95	_____	_____
T-Shirt (XL, XXL)	$14.95	_____	_____
Coffee Mug	$ 9.95	_____	_____
Poster	$ 9.95	_____	_____
Hat (Cap)	$14.95	_____	_____

Shipping & Handling

If Sub Total is:	USA	Canada	
$0 – 25	$5	$10	Sub Total: _____
$25 – 100	$10	$20	S & H _____
$100 – 200	$15	$30	
$200 – 300	$25	$40	Total: _____

- *Call for price on orders over $300*
- *Canadian shipping prices do not include duty, taxes or customs charges that could be charged at the border.*

Name _____ Date _____

Company _____

Street Address _____

City_____ State/Province _____

Zip _____ County _____ Phone _____

Payment Information:

_____ Check/Money Order

_____ American Express _____ Visa _____ Master Card

Credit Card #: _____

Exp Date: _____ Signature: _____

PlatinumStar™ Publishing,

P.O. Box 891, Woodland Hills, California 91365-0891
866.ASK.TONY Office, 818.992.6443 Fax,
www.platinumstar.com
Quantity discounts available on all products